R. D. Bartlett and Patricia P. Bartlett

Chameleons

Everything about Selection, Care,
Nutrition, Diseases, Breeding, and Behavior

With 72 Color Photographs by R. D. Bartlett

Illustrations by Tom Kerr

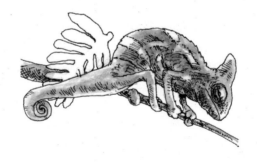

BARRON'S

All inquiries should be addressed to:
Barron's Educational Series, Inc.
250 Wireless Boulevard
Hauppauge, NY 11788

International Standard Book No. 0-8120-9157-4

Library of Congress Catalog Card No. 95-16529

**Library of Congress Cataloging-in-Publication
Data**
Bartlett, Richard D., 1938–
    Chameleons : everything about selection,
  care, nutrition, diseases, breeding, and behavior / R. D. Bartlett and Patricia P. Bartlett ; illustrations by Tom Kerr.
        p.   cm.
    Includes index.
    ISBN 0-8120-9157-4
    1. Chameleons as pets. 2. Chameleons.
  I. Bartlett, Patricia Pope, 1949–   . II. Title.
  SF459.C45B37   1995
  639.3'95—dc20   95-16529
                                          CIP

Printed in Hong Kong

56789   9955   987654321

About the Authors

R. D. Bartlett is a herpetologist who has
authored more than 350 articles and three books
on reptiles. He lectures extensively and has par-
ticipated in field studies across North and Latin
America.

In 1970 he began the Reptilian Breeding and
Research Institute, a private facility. Since its
inception more than 150 species of reptiles and
amphibians have been bred at RBRI, some for
the first time in the United States under captive
conditions. Successes at the RBRI include several endangered species.

Bartlett is a member of numerous herpetological and conservation organizations.

Patricia Bartlett received her B.S. from Colorado
State University and became the editor for an
outdoors book publishing firm in St. Petersburg,
Florida. Subsequently, she worked for the science
museum in Springfield, Massachusetts and was
director of the historical museum in Ft. Myers,
Florida. She is the author of five books on natural
history and historical subjects.

Photos on the Covers

Front: *Chamaeleo calyptratus*
Inside front: *Bradypodion fischeri fischeri*
Inside back: *Furcifer petteri*
Back: *Calumma parsonii*

Important Note

Before using any of the electrical equipment
described in this book, be sure to read
Avoiding Electrical Accidents on page 26.

While handling chameleons you may occasionally receive bites or scratches. If your skin
is broken, see your physician immediately.

Some terrarium plants may be harmful to
the skin or mucous membranes of human
beings. If you notice any signs of irritation,
wash the area thoroughly. See your physician
if the condition persists.

Chameleons may transmit certain infections
to humans. Always wash your hands carefully
after handling your specimens. Always supervise
children who wish to observe your chameleons.

Contents

Without collecting data, many chameleons can be difficult to identify. This pretty female is probably a Chamaeleo bitaeniatus.

Preface

As mankind continues to reduce the already significantly diminished wild areas of our world, we come in fleeting contact with smaller woodland and wildland creatures. Among these are the wonderful and highly specialized lizards we call chameleons. Sadly, some species will be "discovered" and extirpated before we even realize that we have found them. But happily many others will remain, at least temporarily, and from these we can continue to learn.

Today, chameleons are appearing with ever-increasing frequency in the pet marketplace. All too often it is not realized until it is too late to save them, that, when kept as "pets," these largely solitary lizards require a regimen of husbandry quite different from that of other lizards.

Within these pages we will introduce you, step by step, to the insights and methods which we and others have successfully used. Probably most important is an understanding of chameleon behavior, especially their relationships with each other and their reaction to stress. When we began in herpetology, the concept of lizards reacting emotionally was unknown; now it is critical to chameleon care.

This book includes sections on selecting a healthy animal, how to house and feed it, recognizing and treating diseases, and breeding requirements. The species accounts will give you information on different kinds of chameleons and their specific needs. Obviously, a chameleon from a mountainous region will need different day/night temperatures than one from sea level, and a decidedly asocial chameleon species cannot be placed where it can even see other members of its own kind.

Chameleons are not creatures that should be purchased on impulse. To realize success with them, the keeper must have dedication and knowledge. It is our hope that this book will help you achieve both.

Acknowledgements

There are many who deserve somewhat more than just a word of thanks for the kindnesses they have provided. Except for the free-living Jackson's chameleons in Hillsborough County, Florida, we have never visited any in the wild. But, because of the friendship and kindness of Bill Love and Rob MacInnes of Glades Herp, Inc., we have had opportunity to photograph and observe more than 40 species of these amazing and interesting species.

Bert and Hester Langerwerf took time to explain the intricacies of their breeding programs for Mid-Natal dwarf chameleons, and we exchanged many notes regarding our respective programs with veiled chameleons.

Sean McKeown has discussed the Jackson's chameleons in Hawaii, and Ken Kalisch was kind enough to share with us a little of his insight regarding the beautiful but problematic Parson's chameleon. Thanks to both.

We especially wish to thank Fredric L. Frye, DVM, both for his contributions in the field of reptile husbandry and for his thoughtful commentary on this book.

Understanding Chameleons

Lizards that are capable of changing their colors have always been of interest to humans. Among those best known for this ability are the Old World "true" chameleons and the New World anoles. (The latter are often, but erroneously, referred to as "American chameleons"; however, they are not even closely related to true chameleons.)

Chameleon count: The known species of true chameleons number about 120. The exact numbers are arguable, for not all taxonomists agree on the exact criteria that define a species. To further complicate mat-ters, new species are discovered and described from time to time.

The source: The island of Madagascar seems to be the cradle of speciation for the true chameleons. Located on the east rim of the Mozambique Channel, the island lies opposite the southern African country of Mozambique. Surrounded by the warm waters of the Indian Ocean, this interesting country of 228,000 square miles boasts more than 60 species of chameleons. Other species abound throughout tropical Africa, fewer are found in North Africa, only two on the Indian subcontinent, and two in Europe.

What Makes a Chameleon Unique

Color

Chameleons are, perhaps, best known for their color-changing abili-ties. Over time this ability, not shared equally by all of the 120 or so chameleon species, has been so exaggerated that we actually expect to see the lizards clad in a perpetually changing kaleidoscope of colors and patterns, or so perfectly matching an artificially gaudy background that they are virtually invisible. Not all chameleons can change their color. But for those species capable of it, color changes have a very distinct function. Those chameleons that change their colors literally "speak with their skins."

Triggers: The color changes are physiological. They are a complex but

Although Madagascar is the "heart" of chameleon speciation, many species are also found in Africa, India, and Southern Europe.

effective method of intraspecific communication. Stress (be it caused by territorial disputes with others of their own kind, adverse temperatures, injury, or any of numerous other reasons) and activity induce chameleons to assume darker colors and more intricate, or at least better-defined patterns. Quiescent specimens experiencing optimum conditions are generally of lighter coloration and display weaker patterns, or are patternless.

Color and sex: There may be significant differences between the day-to-day colorations of male and female chameleons. Gravid female chameleons often assume and retain colors and/or patterns unlike those displayed at any other time in their lives.

Color and range: Geographical range is another factor in determining color. Many chameleon species exhibit rather noticeable color and pattern variations within the extremes of their range.

The most varied: When all factors pertaining to color and pattern change are considered, it is the wide ranging common chameleon, *Chamaeleo chamaeleon*, that is the most variable of all. More than one hundred color and pattern variations have been recorded for it.

Anatomy

Many species of chameleons are bizarrely adorned with casques, flaps, and hornlike nasal appendages on their heads. Some also have sail-like vertebral crests on their backs and/or tails.

Unlike many other lizards, which are either basically round or horizontally flattened, true chameleons are flattened vertically. Unlike *any* other lizards, chameleons have their toes wrapped into opposing units—two on one side of each foot, three on the other. With tonglike action, the toes tightly grip the branches of trees and shrubs as the chameleon moves

slowly about. The tails of arboreal species (which includes most chameleons) are also strongly prehensile. At rest, they are often held coiled like a watch spring.

The skin: As they grow, chameleons shed their skin periodically. Shedding occurs more frequently when the lizard is growing rapidly. The skin is most usually shed in patchwork fashion, with ultimately the entire skin, including the eyelids and toes, being shed.

The eyes: The eyes of a healthy chameleon are protuberant, turretlike, and have the lids fused except for a central aperture through which the pupil peers. Working independently of each other, the animal may be scanning rearward for an approaching enemy with one eye while watching the front or side for insect prey with the other.

When prey is sighted, the chameleon stalks slowly, haltingly forward, until about one body-length away from its intended prey. The two eyes are then directed toward the insect, thus creating binocular vision. Slowly the chameleon opens its mouth and shoots its tongue forward. In an instant the insect has disappeared and the lizard is munching contentedly.

The tongue: It is the mechanism that caused the insect to disappear, the chameleon's tongue structure, that is of so much interest to reptile enthusiasts. No other lizard has quite the same arrangement. So different is the chameleon's tongue structure that these lizards were once placed in their own suborder, the Rhiptoglossa. This translates, literally, to "whip-tongue." By the simultaneous contraction of numerous muscles, the tongue, often nearly as long as the body and head of the lizard, is projected quickly forward. The thickened tip has a central indentation as well as mucous-secreting glands. The prey insect is

This is a rather typically colored male panther chameleon, Furcifer pardalis.

A pair of Chamaeleo jacksonii xantholophus *in profile.*

both gently grasped by and "glued" to the tongue tip of the chameleon. The tongue, insect secured, is then retracted. When fully retracted the tongue surrounds a projection of one of the hyoid bones. Once in the chameleon's strong jaws, the prey is methodically and thoroughly masticated, then swallowed. So effective is this arrangement that larger species of chameleons have been known to capture small rodents and birds.

Size

How big do chameleons get? Their sizes vary tremendously. Males of many species are larger than the females. The smallest species, the pygmy leaf chameleon from Madagascar, as an adult is only an inch and a half in length (3–8 cm). The largest, also of Madagascar, is a gigantic morph of the already normally large Oustalet's chameleon. This Brobdignagian creature can exceed 30 inches (76 cm) in overall length.

Reproduction

Although most chameleons are egg-layers (oviparous), some, especially those from high altitudes, are live-bearers (ovoviviparous). Chameleons breed at early ages, have large numbers of eggs or young, and seem to have relatively short life spans in the wild.

Sexing your chameleon: Most chameleons show sexual differences (sexual dimorphism). The males often display prominent secondary characteristics such as horns, rostral protuberances, or crests. Males are also often larger than the females. Sex-linked related color differences may also occur in some species. In those species which do not exhibit overt sexual differences, gender can often be determined by examining the base of the tail immediately posterior to the

Juvenile Furcifer minor *are not brightly colored.*

cloaca. If the specimen is a male, a bilateral swelling caused by the hemipenes may often be seen.

Thermoregulation

Thermoregulation simply means "temperature regulation." When applied to reptiles, the term refers to a specimen keeping its body temperature within a suitable range. Reptiles (except for the marine leatherback turtle) are entirely poikilothermic. This means that the body temperature of a reptile is regulated by external environmental factors rather than internal mechanisms.

To maintain necessary bodily functions a reptile (chameleons included) must maintain its body temperature within certain specified upper and lower levels. The necessary parameters may vary considerably by species. Species adapted to high elevations or other cooler climates are fully functional at considerably cooler body temperatures than a lowland rainforest species would be. But each must strive to maintain that suitable temperature. Body temperatures either too hot or too cold can be debilitating or even fatal.

How it's done: A cold chameleon increases its body temperature by positioning itself, sides flattened and tilted, against the warming rays of the sun. When faster warming is desired, the chameleon darkens its color somewhat and lessens the volume of air contained in its lungs. Conversely, techniques used by a hot chameleon to reduce its body temperature include facing into the sun (thus presenting less body surface to absorb the warmth), moving into the shade, lightening its body color, and panting. Thus, not only is absorption of heat reduced, but panting causes moisture evaporation from the mucous membranes, which actually cools the lizard.

Coping with extremes: Chameleon species that live in regions where adverse seasonal temperatures occur have developed methods of protecting themselves from the extremes. Two such methods are *brumation* and *aestivation.* Brumation pertains to a winter dormancy; aestivation, to summer dormancy.

Chameleons from high altitudes (or other areas that experience a significant drop in winter temperatures) brumate. Chameleons from the hot tropical lowlands may aestivate during periods of excessive warmth or drought.

In both cases the lizards usually burrow beneath yielding substrates for their periods of dormancy. However, some species found in areas that become cold but do not freeze may simply become quiescent while clinging to a branch.

Both brumation and aestivation may last for a period of several weeks.

The Solitary Chameleon

By nature chameleons are either preferentially solitary or found in pairs. It would appear that while none are communal animals, some are more tolerant of the presence of conspecifics and closely related species than others.

Pairs or trios: In captivity, if given sufficient space, most species of chameleons can be kept in pairs or trios. However, groups of chameleons that have been compatible in large cages may no longer be so if changed to smaller quarters. You must continually monitor the interactions of all members of the group.

Stress: Be aware of the effects of low level stress. Even if not overt, the dominance factor can prevent subordinate specimens from feeding, drinking, or resting normally or sufficiently. Monitor your groups continually. Chameleons that are compatible when not sexually active may become formidable adversaries when sexually mature or sexually active. It is seldom possible to keep two sexually mature males together. Antagonism between adult males is almost a certainty. (I have not noticed antagonistic behavior in colonies of leaf chameleons, but this is just my finding. It may not pertain in all cases or with all species.)

Agonism (antagonism, unease) between male chameleons will be manifested most noticeably by rapid color changes, lateral flattening of the body, head bobbing, gaping, pursuit, and actual skirmishing. Males of closely allied species will fight as persistently as males of the same species. However, head bobbing and nodding and color changes may also indicate courtship when used by a male in the presence of a female.

Breeding hostility: In the normal course of breeding activities, the males (the larger sex in most chameleon species) may seriously injure the female. Be ready to intervene and cage the animals separately if necessary.

The Chameleon Family

All chameleons (better termed "chameleonids") belong to the family Chamaeleonidae, which consists of two subfamilies: the "typical" and the dwarf chameleons, which are contained in the subfamily Chamaeleoninae; and the "atypical" (or basically terrestrial) leaf chameleons, which are members of the subfamily Brookesiinae.

In turn, each of these two groups is divided into different genera, each with its own characteristics. The genera contained in the first subfamily are *Chamaeleo*, (this genus is currently broken into two related groups, *Chamaeleo* and *Trioceros*), *Bradypodion*, *Calumma* and *Furcifer*. The Brookesiinae contains the genera *Brookesia* and *Rhampholeon*.

Chamaeleoninae: The members of the subfamily Chamaeleoninae move more quickly and with more dexterity, are more arboreal, more capable of changing color, have a smoother skin and a proportionately longer, more prehensile tail than their predominantly terrestrial, leaflike cousins. Some can be quite aggressive towards their own and other species.

Members of the four genera of the subfamily Chamaeleoninae have unicuspid claws on each toe and prehensile tails. There are both oviparous and ovoviviparous species in this subfamily.

Brookesiinae: The leaf chameleons (also called "stump-tailed chameleons") of the subfamily Brookesiinae are characterized by their slow movements, their relatively benign dispositions, and their lack of color changes. Members of this family have bicuspid claws. Additionally, the tails of these little chameleons are only weakly or completely nonprehensile. Most of these chameleons have a complex scalation which features dorsolateral projections, spinous body scales, and supraorbital projections. They are small lizards, with a body length of slightly more than 1 to 4 inches (2.54–10.16 cm) in length.

A Quick Lesson in Taxonomy

Taxonomy is the science of classifying organisms. To arrive at proper classifications, the biological and morphological characteristics of living organisms are considered. The process starts in a generalized manner but quickly becomes very detailed.

Following a taxonomic classification is rather simple and yet very enlightening. Here is the method and terminology used for scientific identification of the spectacular veiled chameleon:

Kingdom Animalia (animal)

Phylum Chordata (vertebrate—an animal with a backbone)

Class Reptilia (reptile—the group containing chelonians [turtles, tortoises], crocodilians [alligators, crocodiles, and allies], rhynchocephalians [tuataras], and squamata)

Some female veiled chameleons, Chamaeleo calyptratus, *have very well developed casques.*

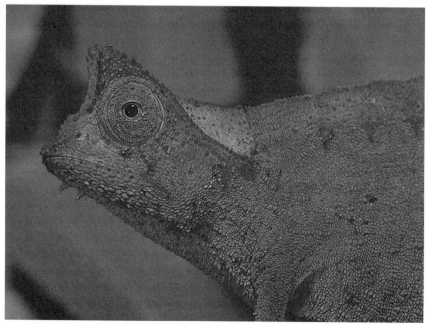

Brookesia superciliaris *is one of the larger and more frequently seen of the leaf chameleons.*

The Family Chamaeleonidae

Subfamily	Genus	Subgenus
Chamaeleoninae	*Chamaeleo*	*Chamaeleo, Trioceros*
	Bradypodion	
	Calumma	
	Furcifer	
Brookesiinae	*Brookesia*	
	Rampholeon	

Order Squamata (the group containing snakes, amphisbaenids, and, lizards)

Suborder Lacertilia (lizard)

Family Chamaeleonidae (chameleonid)

Subfamily Chamaeleoninae (typical and dwarf chameleons)

Genus *Chamaeleo* (typical chameleon)

Species *calyptratus* (veiled chameleon)

Subspecies *calyptratus* (nominate or first-described race)

As we can see from the above example, the taxonomic position of the veiled chameleon is precise, and its identification is easily ascertained by researchers across the world. It is the morphology, the biology, and the characteristics of the lizard that makes such precise classification possible. What are some of these characteristics? The fact that the creature is animate makes it an animal. Its backbone makes it a vertebrate. The dry, scaly skin and the fact that it is poikilothermic (cold-blooded) defines it as a reptile. We can easily see that it is a lizard, and the prehensile tail, bundled toes, turreted eyes, and laterally flattened body further tells us it is a chameleonid.

The classification of chameleons and the scientific names which have been given them (and all other animals and plants) are the results of careful consideration by taxonomists. Since each taxonomist places special emphasis on his or her particular discipline, the views on exact classification may differ somewhat. Still, at present these are the closest thing we have to uniformity. With time additional uniformity will likely be realized.

A genus (plural, genera) is a grouping of related species with similar characteristics. As mentioned earlier, I recognize six genera of chameleons. Other persons may recognize fewer or more.

The term "species" designates a group of creatures exhibiting the same characteristics, living in the same biotope, and whose offspring are fertile.

The designation "subspecies" represents a population geographically isolated from the species and which presents specific genetic characters different from the species type. Successful breedings between subspecies are possible.

HOW-TO:
Identifying a Chameleon

Head

Well defined; wider than neck.

Eye: Proportionately huge, roundly protruding. Lids fused except for pupillary opening. Capable of independent motion and vision. Both eyes focus on prey when feeding.

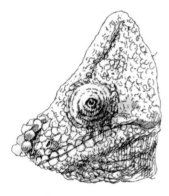

Calumma globifer.

Rostral (nose) area: Variable; may be adorned by single nonrigid, laterally flattened "paddle" (*C. nasuta*); single rigid, flattened, or conical structure (*B. carpenteri, C. melleri*); single barely noticeable, scaled ridge (*F. pardalis*); two rigid, laterally flattened structures (*B. fischeri*); two annulated hornlike structures (*C. montium*); two rigid, scaled structures (*C. parsonii*); three annulated hornlike structures (*C. jacksonii*); six small to medium structures of graduated size (*C. quadricornis*); no adornment (*C.calyptratus*).

Calumma gallus *(top)*, C. gastrotaenia *(center)* and C. boettgeri *(bottom)* display three different nose styles within a single genus.

Crown: Single casque; occipital lobes (flaps); various crests (parietal, temporal, supraorbital, lateral).

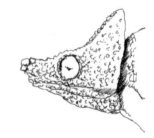

Casque styles also vary by species as displayed by Furcifer oustaleti *(top)*, Calumma cucullata *(center)*, and Calumma p. parsonii *(bottom)*.

Tongue: Complex, protrusible, from slightly less to considerably more than the body length.

Now you see it, now you don't: the chameleon using its tongue to catch an insect.

Gular Area: Typical chameleons: Inflatable; often with serrate gular crest on throat. Leaf chameleons: Not so inflatable. Gular crests lacking.

Chameleons with inflatable gular areas (top) use them to signify territoriality. Those without inflatable gulars rely on other types of body language (bottom).

Body
Laterally compressed; with or without dorsal and/or ventral crests.

The presence or absence of dorsal and ventral crests can help identify a chameleon species.

Limbs: Four; slender but strongly muscled.
Toes: Opposable; fused into twos or threes for all but their tips. All toes have claws. The claws of the typical chameleons are unicuspid (single tip); those of the leaf chameleons are bicuspid (two tips).

Pincer-like toes provide a strong grip for arboreal species.

Tail: Typical chameleons: Strongly prehensile. Leaf chameleons: Weakly or completely nonprehensile.

Prehensile or not, tails are important balancing tools for chameleons.

15

Acquiring a Chameleon

Chameleons in the Pet Market

Although many species of chameleons are diminishing in numbers and some populations are seriously depleted, none are yet considered threatened or endangered under the criteria of the Endangered Species Act.

However, the exportation of all chameleons is regulated by CITES (Convention for International Trade in Endangered Species) and many are entirely protected by the countries to which they are indigenous.

Until the very late 1980s, all chameleons available in the pet trade were wild collected imports. This has now changed somewhat—but only somewhat. Today, probably 15 percent of the specimens in the pet trade are captive-bred and born (or hatched). Of these, some are farm-bred in Madagascar and some are the result of captive breeding programs in the United States and Europe.

Out of the wild: What exactly does "farm-raised" signify? In the strictest sense, farm-raised would indicate that the specimens in question have been captive bred and captive hatched. And in all fairness, this sometimes does occur. However, the origins of other baby chameleons are at least slightly tainted, for in many cases breeders still catch and buy gravid females or purchase baby chameleons found hatching in the wild. The eggs of the gravid females are incubated and hatched in captivity. The babies are then mixed with those that are truly captive-bred and -hatched.

To the jobber: The eggs have been laid, incubated, and the hatchlings are emerging from the nests. What happens next?

Orders are received and sorted by the breeders and exporters. The chameleons, both babies and adults, are gathered together and packed (the adults, usually into small, individual cloth bags; the babies, in multiples). Remember that chameleonids are largely solitary creatures that do not like being together.

The bags are then suspended from cross-braces of a big, wooden shipping crate. Exactly how many lizards go into each box depends on the size of the lizards, the crates, and the shipping quotas then in place. The lizards are all transported by air. Airplane bin temperatures at 30,000 feet are heated, but these temperatures are still often well below the minimum ever experienced by chameleons in nature. Such temperatures, even for a short time, induce stress—and stress is a word that will be mentioned time and again in this book.

Once received by the jobber the chameleons are released into holding facilities. At some of the best facilities, the chameleons (at least the more expensive species) are held one per tank. In this manner, their feeding, drinking, and health can best be monitored. At other importers, these asocial creatures are held a dozen or even a hundred to a single holding tank. There is simply no way to monitor feeding, heating, and lighting accurately in these facilities. In many cases, all are subminimal. Again, this results in stress.

To the wholesaler: Then comes the call from the wholesaler: "Send

An elephant-
eared chameleon,
Calumma brevicor-
nis, *at rest.*

me, oh, 50 baby chameleons and, I guess, three dozen pairs of assorted adults." And for the lizards the ordeal starts anew.

This time each of the adults is placed in a cloth bag containing crumpled newspapers and the babies are placed in small cups. The bags are then placed in styrofoam shipping boxes, and the chameleons begin a new journey, winging their ways northward (most jobbers are in southern California or Florida). Again, temperatures are usually suboptimal and the chameleons may be in their darkened shipping containers for two full days. More stress.

To the pet store: But it's not over yet! The same ordeal occurs again to get the chameleons from the wholesalers to the individual pet shops. (Have I mentioned stress yet?) The initial care given these stressed lizards by the pet shop employees is very critical to the future well-being of the reptiles. They need solitude, warm temperatures, rehydrating, vitamins and minerals, and ample feedings of nutritious food right away. Denied any of these at the shop, the condition of the lizards will deteriorate more rapidly and may quickly become irreversible.

To the hobbyist: Then comes the final consumer, the hobbyist—past, present, or future—who usually looks with open-eyed wonder at the chameleons (chameleons have that effect on almost everybody) and who often becomes infatuated with their prehistoric appearance. The purchase is often one of impulse, with no advance preparation or research of any kind having been made. And it is for *you* that this booklet is intended.

So You Want to Own a Chameleon?

Many questions are usually asked when one first encounters a chameleon. One of the first is "Can this thing be real?" Following that first question, a series of others usually follows. "Will it live? How do you take care of it? Where does it come from? If it lives, does it make a good pet?"

A tricky undertaking: Unfortunately, the chances of most chameleons surviving for extended periods in captivity are not at all good. This is sad, but very true. Stress contributes markedly to debilitation. With chameleons, nearly anything can induce stress. And once the health of a chameleon has deteriorated to a point at which problems are observable, it is very difficult to reverse the down slide that will ultimately result in the death of the lizard. With this in mind, it then becomes obvious that if you are thinking about the purchase of a chameleon, you *must* initially select one in top-notch condition and then strive to keep it that way.

Get a good start: Purchase your chameleon from a *reputable* and *knowledgeable* source. Unfortunately, many pet shop employees know precious little about reptilian husbandry. This is most easily reflected by the suboptimal conditions in which they keep their lizards. Find a pet shop with employees who can answer your questions accurately. To determine accuracy, compare some of their answers to your questions to the information contained in this book. They should jibe. If the pet-shop employees can not answer your questions satisfactorily, the chances are excellent that they are not caring for their chameleons properly.

If the chameleons in the shop are housed several to a cage or crowded into a cage with other lizard species, the store's husbandry techniques are flawed and other information may also be. Shop elsewhere.

Find a veterinarian who is well versed in reptile husbandry and health. You will quite likely need his or her services sooner or later (and unfortunately it will more often than not be sooner). The treatment of reptiles is a specialty practice. Not all veterinarians will be able to diagnose and treat an ailing chameleon.

Prepare the caging for your chameleon in advance. The chances are excellent that you will be purchasing a (somewhat) stressed lizard. It must have a cage in which it can feel secure awaiting its arrival.

Once all of these factors are in place, you are ready to acquire a chameleon.

Important note: Support domestic herpetocultural and conservation efforts. Buy chameleons that have been captive-bred and -hatched whenever possible.

These might be a little more expensive than imports, but purchasing domestically produced chameleons, captive-bred and -hatched young, will help assure that you have a specimen either parasite-free or with a minimum parasite load. Because the insects consumed by *all* chameleons, either wild or domestically produced, carry parasites, there may not be a truly parasite-free chameleon. However, since captive-produced chameleons are usually not only less stressed, but are less easily stressed than wild specimens, they are apt to be in better overall condition. Additionally, the purchase of captive-bred/captive-hatched chameleons is a valid conservation tool, reducing the draw on wild chameleon populations.

Choosing a Healthy Chameleon

Even the easiest to keep of the true chameleons are difficult in comparison with many other lizard species. This makes it even more important that you

start with a healthy animal. Here's what to look for:
• Purchase captive-born or -hatched specimens whenever possible.
• If no captive-produced chameleon is available, accept only well-acclimated animals.
• Many importers now routinely test and treat freshly imported chameleons for internal parasites. Try to ascertain that this has been done.
• The specimen must have good body weight. Do not purchase one that has the ribs, shoulder, or pelvic girdles strongly evident.
• The lizard must appear alert.
• The pupil opening must be round with no encrustations on the lids. The eyes should be protuberant, not sunken.
• The lizard should not have any swellings on toes, legs, tail, or body.
• The specimen should not be gasping or breathing with opened mouth.
• There should be no swellings, redness, or scabs on the lips.
• Many chameleons have subcutaneous parasites and worms. These are visible as raised welts. Do not purchase a chameleon on which these are visible.
• Try to choose chameleons that have been housed individually.
• Immediately take your newly purchased animal to a reptile veterinarian for an overall checkup and fecal exam. Treat as necessary.

My tip: Of the two chameleon groups, the members of the terrestrial short-tailed chameleon group (*Brookesia* and *Rhampholeon*) seem to resent handling less than most of the arboreal species. However, *none* likes it. *As a generality, chameleons should be considered display lizards that should not be handled.*

Housing

Caging Types

Wood and Wire Caging

Enclosure size: It is my preference to provide chameleons with the largest possible enclosures. Those that I use most frequently measure overall 48 × 30 × 71 inches (121 × 76 × 180 cm). All are on large casters (wheels) to facilitate easy moving. The uprights of the frames and the door assembly are made from two-by-twos. The top and bottom are solid pieces of marine plywood. The top has had the center removed, leaving a rim about 6 inches wide all the way around. The sides, front, back, door, and top are covered

Large, heavily planted, wood and wire cages have proven excellent facilities for most chameleons.

with ⅛ inch (0.3 cm) mesh hardware cloth that is stapled tightly in place. The 30-inch width and the 71-inch height (which includes the casters) allow these cages to be easily wheeled through average interior and exterior doorways. Thus, it is a simple matter to wheel the cages outside on nice days, to allow the chameleons to partake of natural sunlight and rain. The cage furniture consists of a full-height ficus tree (usually *F. benjamina*) and a number of dead-limb perches of suitable diameter.

Cool weather: If left outdoors during cool weather, the cages are wrapped in clear 4-mil plastic sheeting. This is stapled in place on three sides, but can be rolled up and out of the way or removed from the top and south side (door side) if desired. A heat lamp is activated when necessary. To ensure the comfort of the lizards, except for the removable front and top, the vinyl can (and probably should) remain in place throughout the winter months. During cool weather, chameleons will spend hours basking in the sunshine. The bottom can be left bare or a low frame can be installed that will retain a clean sand substrate. (While I do use sand on the bottoms of my cages, I merely pile it high in the cage center and let it seek its own level—including being washed out—during storms.)

Smaller cages: While the large step-in cages described above are my preference, especially for such large species as veiled, Oustalet's, Parson's, and Meller's chameleons, I have used smaller cages equally well for both large and small species. I have successfully kept small chameleon species such as carpets, Petter's, and others of similar size, in wood and wire cages that measured 24 × 18 × 36 inches (60 × 45 × 90 cm). A potted shrub of some type as well as horizontal limbs for perching have always been incorporated into the decor. Obviously, these smaller cages can easily be carried outside in warm weather and inside in cooler weather.

Ground dwellers: For forest-floor chameleons, such as the interesting little leaf chameleons (genera *Brookesia* and *Rhampholeon*), and for the common chameleon (the most terrestrial member of the genus *Chamaeleo*) the height can be lessened by 50 percent or more (to 12 or 18 inches; 30–45 cm).

I prefer caging of wood and wire construction, as chameleons prefer well ventilated quarters with no standing moisture. It is easier to accomplish such a habitat with wood and wire cages than it is with glass terraria. The use of ⅛-inch mesh in the cage construction will keep all but the smallest food insects from escaping. Although this mesh size is smaller than many hobbyists use, I have never had any broken toes or toenail trauma within my collection.

Some researchers recommend that only plastic-coated wire be used, to avoid abrasion of snout or foot damage. Whichever type you choose, it is important to use only smooth-surfaced wire.

Other Types of Terraria

Using aquariums: There are times and places when decor and/or space constraints make wood and wire cages impractical. For those circumstances there are hosts of commercially constructed or home-made aquariums that double admirably as terrariums.

Horizontal or vertical: When figuring just how you're going to adapt your

Round hanging cages can be placed unobtrusively in the garden.

aquarium tank, always consider the proposed residents. For arboreal chameleons, the height of the terrarium provided should be of as much consideration as the floor space. If it is terrestrial chameleons which you are housing, then, of course, the height of the cage is far less important.

A suitable top (or front, as the case may be) will need to be provided. With the standard orientation this poses no problem. However, when the upright orientation is preferred, formulating an escape-proof front becomes more difficult. This may be approached from two angles. Firstly, if not *too* heavy, a glass front may be cut and held in position with a hinge of silastic aquarium sealant. A hook and hasp may be similarly held in place on the opposite side. I have found that if the edge of the glass door rests flush against the table or stand top (or the inside glass of the aquarium) the sealant hinge is much less stressed. The second method is to

A large movable cage that has been provided with heat lamps and a watering drip bucket. This type of cage can be adapted for woodland or savanna habitat.

sit your terrarium an inch or two off the flat surface on blocks or legs. A tightly fitting framed front can then simply be slipped over the open side.

Habitats

There are two basic habitats that may be replicated in caging. Both can have both terrestrial and arboreal applications.

Savanna Terrarium

Savannas defined: Savannas are areas of transition between or at the edge of forest, woodland, or desert. The treed and sunlit edges of these spacious, rolling, otherwise sparsely vegetated glades are the habitats of many chameleon species. Different soil formation and moderated rainfall provide a habitat much different from that of either surrounding desert or woodland/forest. Savannas often host various species of moderately, or at least seasonally lush grasses, as well as thornscrub and other formidably armed trees. Areas of rocky scree may

be present. A dry savanna will work well for the desert chameleon species.

Savannas are often subjected to weather extremes in the form of temperature, rainfall, or other such climatic vagaries. The plant community found in savannas is difficult to maintain in terraria over extended periods. Periodic refurbishing of your terrarium vegetation will most likely be necessary.

Basics: A thick layer of sandy humus into which a liberal helping of variably sized rocks have been mixed should comprise the substrate of the savanna terrarium. Seedling acacias and clumped grasses, as well as weathered branches, cactus skeletons, and strategically placed rocks and rock formations can be used for decorative purposes. The savanna terrarium plant community will require somewhat more water than those in the desert terrarium. However, even with judicious care, many (especially the grasses) will need replacing each season. The plants can be either potted or planted directly into the terrarium substrate. I prefer the latter, simply for aesthetics. A screen top will assist you in keeping the lower humidity preferred by most savanna-dwelling chameleon species.

Woodland/Forest Terrarium

Woodland defined: Woodland/forest terraria can be utilized for those chameleons of humid, rainy montane and tropical origins. Because of the host of easily grown potted houseplants and scientifically formulated soils that are available, woodland/forest terraria are among the most easily constructed and maintained of the various terrarium types. Besides the plants, attractive branches and rocks work well as decorative and functional objects in the woodland/forest terrarium. To maintain your plants successfully, it will be necessary to ensure that their roots remain damp but not soggy, and to provide them with adequate lighting. Even shade-tolerant philodendrons, pothos, and syngoniums will require several hours of fairly strong light daily if they are to survive.

Basics: When constructing a woodland terrarium, I suggest first placing an inch or two of pea-sized gravel as the base of the substrate. On top of this I lay a thickness or two of air-conditioning filter material cut to the exact size of terrarium. This latter prevents the two or three inches of soil that comes next from filling the spaces between the gravel. The rocks below the filter material act as a reservoir that will prevent excess water from destroying the roots of your plants if you should happen to overwater. Of course, if you regularly overwater, or overwater too excessively, the reservoir will become filled and provide little benefit to the setup.

Some terrarium keepers prefer a simplified approach. With this, several inches of commercially available wood mulch (cypress, aspen, etc., but *not* cedar) is used as the substrate and the plants that are used remain in their pots, merely being sunk to the pot rim in the mulch. This is an easily cleaned arrangement. The mulch can be washed, sterilized, dried, and reused.

A glass or plastic top will help retain the high humidity preferred by many of the denizens of these habitats. If the humidity remains too high it can be reduced by substituting a screen, or a combination screen and glass cover for the full glass one.

Cage Furnishings

Cage furnishings for chameleons can be both functional and decorative.
- Among the primarily functional examples are such items as the new-to-the-market heating "limbs."
- Some of the more terrestrial chameleons seem to enjoy clamber-

Horizontal caging is best for terrestrial or ground-dwelling species.

ing about on rock formations, prone limbs, etc.
- Sturdy vining plants and elevated limbs will provide both perches and visual barriers as well as adding beauty to the terrarium.
- Attractive pieces of dried (sometimes bleached or sandblasted) manzanita, grape, or other gnarled woods, are often available at pet shops or from the wild.

If multilayered rock formations are provided, the rocks should be held in

Vertical caging is preferred by arboreal, or tree-dwelling chameleons.

Brookesia ebenaui, *a leaf chameleon from Madagascar, occasionally is available in the pet trade.*

place (and together) with a nontoxic adhesive. Latex aquarium sealant is quite satisfactory for this purpose. If even a single flat rock is placed on the surface of the sand it should be ascertained that it cannot accidentally shift and injure your chameleon. Natural rocks provide better clawholds for your specimens than the decorative glass rocks do. If misted, rocks, limbs, and vegetation can all provide drinking stations for your chameleons.

Terrarium Cleanliness

Terrarium cleanliness is one of the most important aspects of successful chameleon husbandry. The substrate should be changed or washed frequently, the perches should be scraped and washed as necessary (or discarded), and all hard surfaces, such as rocks and glass, cleaned and sterilized. Water, whether in bowls (with aereators) or in daily mistings, *must* be fresh and clean.

Fortunately, chameleons are not particularly messy animals. Keeping a chameleon cage clean is usually rather easy. To sterilize perches, twigs, rocks, cork bark, and the terrarium itself, a diluted solution of either Ro-Cal or chlorine bleach should be used. After cleaning and sterilizing the items, be sure all are thoroughly rinsed with clean, fresh water.

Warning: Do not use pine oils or other phenol-based disinfectants for cleaning your chameleon cage. Phenols are absorbed through the skin. *Even lingering odors can be deleterious.*

Terrarium cleanliness will do much to ensure the long-term good health of your specimens. Regular cleaning will help prevent the spread of both diseases and parasites. The cleaning of terraria should be a prominent part of your husbandry regimen.

Spiny chameleons, Furcifer verrucosus, *often display at least a little green on their sides.*

Lighting and Heating

Temperature Requirements

As mentioned previously, the temperatures at which chameleons are comfortable—and the temperatures you will need to offer in your caging—vary according to species. Desert/dry savanna species, such as the veiled or the North African subspecies of the common chameleon, prefer warmer temperatures but lower humidity than montane forest species such as the Jackson's or Elliot's chameleons. The desert forms are even able to withstand temperatures as high as 95°F (35°C) with no ill effects. High-altitude species would be quickly and noticeably distressed by such warmth. Nighttime temperatures can be (in fact, should be) somewhat cooler than daytime highs for all chameleons.

To provide your chameleon with the temperatures necessary for its well-being, it is necessary to know something about your specimen. Suggestions for many are provided in the species account section of this book. If you are unsure of what temperature your species prefers, I suggest erring on the cool end of the spectrum but providing a warmed and illuminated basking area.

A cage that is maintained in the low seventies F (21°–23°C) by day and in the low sixties F (16°–18°C) by night will prove ideal for many chameleon species. Provide a warmed basking area (surface temperature of 88°F [31°C]) during the hours of daylight by prudent use of a floodlight. Except in the case of the few terrestrial chameleon species that will bask on the ground, the warmed basking area should be a suitably sized, elevated limb.

Light Can Mean Heat

Terrarium lights can be used not only for their primary purpose of

25

illuminating a cage, but also as a reliable and easily controlled heat source. Rather inexpensive in-line thermostats or rheostats can be installed by electricians. Plug-in timers are readily available at hardware stores.

Other heat sources: Heating pads, heat tapes, and undertank heaters are all easily procured in feed, hardware, or pet stores. By placing one beneath one end of the terrarium you can create a desired thermal gradient.

Ceramic heaters that screw into incandescent sockets are also readily available. Providing warmth from above, they heat the interior of the terrarium but emit no light. If these are used, it will be necessary to also use terrarium lighting during daylight hours.

Light quality: Is full-spectrum (UV-producing) lighting necessary for chameleons? If it isn't absolutely necessary, it is at least *very* beneficial. Two wave lengths of UV are produced by full-spectrum bulbs. These are UV-A and UV-B. UV-A has been shown, time and again, to promote natural behavior in reptiles. The findings are equally favorable for UV-B. This latter stimulates the synthesis of vitamin D_3, the presence of which enhances calcium absorption and metabolization.

So, do chameleons require the beneficial UV rays? Well, in the wild most arboreal species regularly avail themselves of the benefits of UV producing sunlight. Even forest-floor dwellers derive the benefits of UV from reflected sunlight. And with chameleons being as difficult to keep as they are anyway, I feel they should be given every assistance possible.

To benefit the chameleons, the full-spectrum fluorescent bulbs must be located about 12 to 18 inches (30.5–45.7 cm) away from the animals. Thus a basking perch should be strategically situated in the terrarium.

A new generation of full-spectrum incandescent light bulbs was recently developed. However, at present most available incandescents provide only illumination and warmth, not UV.

Natural light: Unfiltered sunlight is unquestionably the best provider of UV. If filtered through regular glass and plexiglass, a great deal of the UV is removed from natural sunlight. Wire-covered wood-frame cages are best suited to take advantage of natural sunlight in outdoor locations.

Warning: Do not place glass or plexiglass terraria in the sunlight. Even in cold weather the glass can concentrate the heat and disable or kill your chameleons.

Caging and Sociability

As mentioned earlier, chameleons are among the most solitary and territorial of lizard species. Some persist (in fact, insist!) in living solitary lives punctuated only by occasional visits with the opposite sex for the sole purpose of breeding. Other species seem to exist in the wild in pairs. Still others might be found in loose groupings consisting of a single male and two or more females. No chameleon species could be considered truly communal.

In captivity, it is usually impossible (and never desirable) to keep more than a single sexually mature male of a given species in each cage. Intraspecific aggression among males can be persistent and fatal.

Once, in an effort to take better advantage of the seasonally waning hours of sunlight, I repositioned two large cages, each holding a trio of veiled chameleons, *Chamaeleo calyptratus*. Each cage was furnished with a small ficus tree, at the top of which the chameleons sunned. For the first day subsequent to the repositioning, I noticed no problems. The cages were separated by 20 feet (6 m) and the views between them from all but the uppermost few inches remained basically obscured.

However, on the second day I noticed that each male was remaining longer than usual at the top of his respective tree. Both remained for long periods in threat postures, and the color of each was brighter than usual. I was puzzled. Could this really be a response by both to the repositioning of the cages? By the afternoon of the second day, when neither male drank when sprayed, I was alarmed. I sat down and watched. Almost as soon as I was quiet both males again clambered to the summits of their trees,

paralleled each other, and began territoriality displays. The problem, and the solution, were now clear. I stapled an opaque divider from the bottom to the top of both cages, and within the hour things were back to normal. By then, both male chameleons had descended somewhat, had drunk, and had accepted food insects. It was a clear case of out of sight, out of mind.

If not crowded, you may usually keep from one to several adult females with each male. Although the females are usually somewhat less aggressive towards each other, hierarchies may be formed. You must ascertain that all subordinate specimens continue to feed and drink adequately, be allowed to bask, and are not unduly stressed by the dominant female. Juveniles of both sexes may be housed together, although growth may be more rapid if but a single specimen is kept per container.

Mixing: It may be possible to keep two diverse species of chameleons together. For instance, I was able to successfully keep a trio of common chameleons and a trio of carpet chameleons together in one of my large step-in cages. The two species showed no interest in each other. Other combinations are likely to be possible. Experiment, but watch closely for adverse reactions.

Certain other herptile species may also be kept with chameleons. Among others are suitably sized anoles, the various species of large day geckos, White's and other large tree frogs, and a fair number of basically terrestrial, nonaggressive lizard species.

Watering and Feeding Your Chameleon

Getting Started

Variety of foods: Although most chameleons are basically insectivorous, some larger species will also prey on the nestlings of mice and small birds. Additionally, at least a few species will consume a fair amount of foliage, flowers, and, occasionally, fruit.

It may take some prompting to get your newly imported chameleon feeding well. Offer it a variety of insects: butterworms, waxworms, giant mealworms, mealworms, crickets, locusts (no lubber grasshoppers though!), roaches, or in the case of baby or small chameleon species, termites. Most chameleons quickly tire of one insect species. Providing an adequate diet can be quite a task, but the life of your lizard depends on it.

Frequency of feeding: Despite their perpetually slow-motion lifestyle, chameleons require daily feedings. In my large step-in cages, this constitutes no problem. I simply maintain a hundred or so crickets (vitamin/mineral-enhanced insect feed is always available in the step-ins) in the cages at all times. In addition, a small number of mealworms or waxworms are offered at intervals. Growing plants are always in the cages. An occasional newly born mouse is also offered. Some breeder chameleons have thrived on such a regimen for more than four years.

In smaller cages, glass terraria, or cages where insect diet is not provided, "gut-loaded" insects are offered

Sweep netting for field plankton.

daily. Those not consumed by the lizards must be removed from the terraria and the insects themselves offered food at the end of the day.

Insects

Insect Care

So your chameleon likes insects—what could be easier? Like other things, there's more to feeding insects than tossing a few odd crickets into the cage. You've got to feed your insects well before you offer them to your chameleons. Offering a poorly nourished insect is a little like feeding bits of chitin; there's not much nutrition in an insect's exoskeleton. A poorly fed or otherwise unhealthy insect offers little but bulk when fed to a chameleon.

My tip: Besides being fed a healthy diet, immediately prior to being fed to the chameleons the insects should occasionally be dusted with a powdered vitamin/mineral supplement. I prefer to do this about twice weekly. I use either RepCAL (a D_3 & Ca supplement) or Osteoform (a broad-spectrum vitamin/mineral supplement). After using both supplements over a period of years, I cannot recommend one above the other.

Feeding food insects: I feel that a mention of "gut-loading" is in order. In this technique your insects are fed an abundance of highly nutritious foods immediately before being offered as food to your chameleons. Calcium, vitamin D_3, fresh fruit and vegetables, fresh alfalfa and/or bean sprouts, honey and vitamin/mineral-enhanced chick-laying mash are only a few of the foods that may be considered in gut-loading your insects.

A commercially prepared gut-loading diet has only recently reached the pet marketplace.

Insect Availability

Except for "field-plankton," all feed-insects, even houseflies, are commercially available. It may be your preference to buy insects. Certainly this is less time-consuming than breeding your own. However, by breeding your own you can ensure that the highest possible diet is continually fed to the insects.

Field Plankton

Availability: Insects straight "from the wild" are already well-fed. These insects have been able to choose their diet and their nutritional value reflects this. Perhaps the very best diet that you can supply your chameleons is that known colloquially as "field plankton" or "field mixture." This is merely a mixture of the various insects and other arachnids that can be field-collected in any given location. To gather them, you simply sweep a suitably meshed field net back and forth through tall grasses or low shrubs after first ascertaining that the area is chemical free.

Having fed "at will" on natural native foods, these insects are probably at their pinnacle of health. Fed immediately after collecting to your chameleons, the health and full guts of the insects will greatly benefit the lizards.

Vegetable Matter

The fresh flowers of nasturtium, hibiscus, dandelion, and rose are often eagerly accepted by chameleons. That these lizards will consume blossoms, and even young leaves, is not well publicized. Do not be afraid to experiment with your chameleons. The diet of some of my large veiled chameleons consists of large amounts of vegetation. Housed in outside "walk-in cages" in which potted shrubs grow, both juveniles and adults of these big chameleons eat considerable quantities of hibiscus and ficus leaves as well as insects and the offered blossoms of other plants. Other chameleon species also eat vegetation.

Subadult panther chameleons, Furcifer pardalis, *are often prominently banded.*

HOW-TO:
Watering Your Chameleon

Most chameleons *do not* recognize standing water as a drinking source. In nature, they either lap the water which condenses and runs down their casque, or they lap dew droplets from leaves. A dish of water at the bottom of their cage is unrecognized as a hydration source. Water must be moving, dangling in droplets from leaves, twigs, or even the terrarium top; or if in a dish, roiled with an air stone to be recognizable.

Acceptable methods of watering your chameleons are:
• Misting (indoors)
• Spraying with a hose (outside cages)
• Drip systems (indoor or outdoor)

Watering with a drip bucket works well for most chameleons.

• Shallow cage-bottom water dish (water roiled by an aquarium air stone)
• Shallow elevated water dish (water roiled by an aquarium air stone)

You may have to try more than one method until you can observe your lizards drinking on a regular basis.

Misting: If you mist or spray the chameleons, direct the spray upward and allow it to fall on the lizards as rain would. I use a spray nozzle and an outside hose to "rain upon" the chameleons in my outside cages. In my indoor cages, I use a simple spray bottle, available at any garden store or at any drugstore. I use tap water and hose water as my water source. The step-in cages are gently sprinkled (twice daily for rainforest species, once daily for desert or savanna species) for a period of several minutes. Each chameleon drinks copiously at nearly every sprinkling.

Drip method: There is a second, almost as effective method of watering the chameleons in these large cages. Several pinhead-sized holes are placed in the bottom of a large plastic bucket. The bucket is then filled with purified water and placed on top of the cage above the tree, while a large "cache-basin" in the form of a big plant saucer is placed on the floor of the cage, underneath the drip area. (You just need to catch most of the drips to help preserve the structural integrity of your cage).

"Moving" the water with an airstone may induce drinking.

The water then drips slowly out of the bucket, falls onto the leaves below, and the chameleons drink the droplets from the leaves. This is another place where the wood/wire construction will stand you in good stead. The water that isn't caught by the basin below the drip bucket merely runs out of the cages, preventing the formation of a quagmire that would be detrimental to the health of your lizard.

The bucket method can also be used in indoor terraria. In an indoor, smaller cage it will be even more important to empty the cachebasin daily.

Water dishes: You could try a water dish on the bottom of your cage, with an air stone inserted into the dish to "move" the water, or you could place this water dish up higher in the cage. Be certain it is firmly seated, so it cannot move, if you place it above cage bottom. This may appeal to lizards that are reluctant to descend to the ground to drink. It should be placed where it is easily reachable from the chameleon's favorite perching area.

Watch your chameleon to make sure that it is drinking, no matter which technique you try.

Your Chameleon's Health

Despite your care in selection, your chameleon may be ill even before you acquire it. New imports may be suffering from something as simple as dehydration. You may need to do more for these than just sprinkle water into their cage. A rehydration chamber is fairly easy to set up, and the results dramatic.

Hydration Chambers

Hydration chambers, long used by zoos and other public institutions, are only now coming into general use by private herpetoculturists and hobbyists. They are especially useful to rehydrate new imports that have become dessicated. A hydration chamber can also be the seasonal trigger for breeding behavior.

Simply put, a hydration chamber provides a recognizable and continuous source of water to the animal. It can be a closed system of high humidity or a wood-and-wire cage with a drip watering system. Which you use depends on your circumstances and the condition of the animal.

Outdoors: In southern Florida, a warm area of ambient high humidity, the latter system worked well for us (and for the animals). New chameleons that were dessicated would spend the majority of their daylight hours hidden among the leaves of the drip-laden ficus, their skins shiny from water droplets, their most evident movement a regular swallowing. As they became rehydrated, the chameleons would begin exploring their cage, sunning

during the day and returning each morning to the top of their cage, near the drip system. If we had lived in an area where outdoor caging was not practical, we would have used a self-contained hydration tank.

Outdoor caging can be modified to a hydration chamber simply by using a mist nozzle on the end of a hose fixed over the cage, and running fresh water through this for an hour or more a day onto the plants within the cage.

Indoors: An indoor hydration chamber can be made from an aquarium, a circulating water pump, branches, and a privacy plant (a small philodendron works well here), a tank heater, a small plastic water bucket with drip holes, and a screen or hardware cloth top.

Hydration chambers provide dessicated chameleons with an opportunity to rehydrate quickly.

The profile of a female globe-horned chameleon, Calumma globifer.

Stand the pump upright in one corner of the tank and lay the heater along the bottom of the tank. Put enough water about 3 inches (7 cm), in the tank to cover the heater and the intake of the recirculating pump. Bend a piece of ½- or ¼-inch hardware cloth to form a false bottom over the water and the heater (you'll have to notch it around the corner pump), so that if your chameleon falls or clambers down, it won't end up in the water. Install the branches and the plant atop the false bottom. Bend a second piece of hardware cloth to form a top, notching if needed for the circulating pump.

Position the small drip bucket adjacent to the pump, and place the outflow of the pump into the drip bucket. If you poke a hole through the bucket to firmly seat the outflow tube, you'll have fewer "fallout" problems.

Plug in the pump and heater, and check the system before you install the lizards. The heater should keep the water at about 80°F (27°C), and the pump should circulate the warmed water from the bottom of the tank into the drip bucket. A continuous warmed flow of "rainwater" should drip from the bucket onto the branches and leaves below. A light can be positioned over the tank to offer illumination and a basking area.

Place your lizard inside the tank and observe it and the tank for a few moments. Needless to say, because you are recirculating the water, it must be changed every time the tank is used. It will do your lizard no good to be doused with contaminated drinking water.

A two- to four-hour period in the hydration tank should do a great deal toward rehydrating your lizard. You may need to give several daily sessions, or until your lizard is no longer dehydrated and, with luck, is feeding well in its own cage. Remember to use fresh water, and keep the tank temperature at about 80°F (27°C), with a warmer basking area.

Respiratory Diseases

The good news is that well-acclimated, properly maintained chameleons are not prone to respiratory ailments. The bad news is that any stressed chameleon, whether a new import, a marginally healthy specimen, or one subjected to unnatural periods of cold (especially humid low temperatures), may break down with a "cold" or pneumonia. Some respiratory infections may also be associated with the weakening brought about by an untenably heavy endoparasitic burden.

Stress, therefore, of one kind or another is usually the culprit to which the origin of a respiratory disease can be traced.

Prevention: We already know that chameleons can be difficult to maintain. Curing a sick one is even more tricky. Here are some suggestions to

lessen the possibility of respiratory illness occurring:
• Cage your chameleon properly; prevent drafts.
• If kept with a cagemate, make sure they are compatible.
• Deparasitize your chameleon.
• Keep the cage temperatures within the norms at all times. In northern climates have a backup system in place.
• Feed a proper diet.

Symptoms: Respiratory ailments are initially accompanied by sneezing, lethargic demeanor and unnaturally rapid, often shallow, breathing.

As the respiratory disorder worsens, rasping and bubbling may accompany each of your chameleon's breaths. At this stage the respiratory infection is often critical and can be fatal.

Treatment: It is mandatory that basking temperatures be elevated during treatment. As soon as a respiratory ailment is suspected, elevate the temperature of your chameleon's basking area to 88° to 94°F (31°–35°C). Do not elevate the temperature of the entire cage, just the basking area. The ambient cage temperature should be 82° to 86°F (27°–29°C). If the symptoms of respiratory distress persist for several hours, the assistance of your reptile vet and antibiotic treatment will be necessary.

There are many "safe" drugs available, but some respiratory diseases do not respond well to these. The newer aminoglycoside drugs are more effective, but correspondingly more dangerous. There is little latitude in dosage amounts and the chameleon *must* be well-hydrated to ensure against kidney damage. The injection site for aminoglycosides must be *anterior* to mid-body to ensure that the renal-portal system is not compromised. It is mandatory that your veterinarian be well acquainted with reptilian medicine to guarantee that the correct decisions are made.

Endoparasites

The presence of internal parasites in wild-caught chameleons is a foregone conclusion. Among others that may be present are roundworms, pin worms, nematodes, filarids, tapeworms, and a whole host of flagellate protozoans.

To treat or not: Although many persons feel wholesale worming of all imported chameleons is a necessity, I feel that whether or not the parasites are combated vigorously should depend on the behavior of the lizard itself. Certainly the problems created by endoparasitic loads in weakened chameleons need be addressed promptly. Will treating a wild import for worms cause it more stress than the presence of the worms themselves? That's a hard question to answer. A fecal exam will have to be run to determine what parasites the chameleon is actually harboring in its gut. Your reptile veterinarian is your best guide in cases like this, but the decision is a judgement call.

However, if the specimen in question is bright-eyed, alert, feeding well, and has good color, you may wish to forego an immediate veterinary assessment. Endoparasitic loads can actually diminish if you keep the cage of your specimen scrupulously clean, thereby preventing reinfestation.

Treatment: Simply stated, the treatment for endoparasites involves administering a potentially toxic substance into the system of your chameleon. Because of this, dosages of the medication must be exact, and even then a weakened lizard might not survive the treatment. Again, I strongly suggest you avail yourself of the services of a knowledgeable veterinarian.

Under the skin: Subcutaneous nematodes are prevalent in many species of chameleons. Many are easily seen as they traverse their routes between the skin and the muscular tissues of the chameleon. They also migrate to and from the gastrointestinal tract. Certain chameleon species seem more susceptible to these parasites than others. Three species among the most commonly imported chameleons that are quite apt to harbor fair numbers of subcutaneous nematodes are the graceful (*C. gracilis*) and the flap-necked (*C. dilepsis*) chameleons of Africa and the panther chameleon (*F. pardalis*) of Madagascar. Avoid any chameleons with these nematode problems. What you are seeing beneath the skin is the proverbial tip of the iceberg.

Ectoparasites

External parasites are less problematic to treat than endoparasites. Only two kinds, ticks and mites, are seen with any degree of regularity. Both ticks and mites feed on the body fluids of their hosts. Both are easily overlooked.

Ticks: These are deflated and seedlike when empty, rounded and bladderlike when engorged. It is best if they are removed singly whenever seen. They embed their mouthparts deeply when feeding, and if merely pulled from the lizard these may break off in the wound. It is best to first dust them individually with Sevin powder or to rub their body parts with rubbing alcohol, then return a few minutes later and pull the ticks gently off with a pair of tweezers.

Mites: Thanks to the advent of No Pest Strips (2.2 dichlorovinyl dimethyl phosphate) mites are easily managed. A small square (approximately ¾ × ¾ inches) placed in the chameleon tank (out of reach of the lizard) for from 12 to 24 hours will usually kill all adult mites. If some survive the initial treatment, treat again a day later. No Pest does not destroy mite eggs. Therefore it will be necessary to repeat the entire treatment nine days later.

Edema/Vitamin A Excess

Just as we thought we were edging ahead of the game in solving chameleon husbandry problems, a new problem—edema—began to manifest itself. Edema is the accumulation of fluids subcutaneously. There are a variety of causes for this in humans, all serious. We don't know that much yet about edema in chameleons, except that it is serious and frequently fatal.

Symptoms: Edema is characterized by goiterlike swellings in the neck and throat. Even long-term captives were developing these symptoms. What was the cause and what could be done? As hobbyists and researchers compared notes, vitamin A became suspect. And, indeed, an excess of vitamin A may well be a contributing cause, or even the primary agent.

But it would appear that vitamin A by itself does not cause the edema. Rather, it would seem that the noticeable fluid pockets are the result of organ dysfunction. The kidneys, the liver, and the heart have all been suggested. Thus, the edema is an outwardly visible symptom of a far more serious underlying problem.

It would seem that an excess of supplemental vitamins (perhaps A, perhaps A *and* others) does figure in the problem somewhere. And since an excess of vitamin A is known to cause liver and kidney damage, it might behoove herpetoculturists to reduce the amount of A offered supplementally. Do not eliminate vitamin A completely; remember that a lack of vitamin A is also fatal. Administer your vitamin/mineral supplements wisely. As a matter of fact, gut-loading your feed insects with beta-carotene rich foods may be the best way of all to supply vitamin A to your chameleons.

Breeding Chameleons

Reproduction: The Function of Color

Emotions: True chameleons depend on their color-changing abilities to advertise many emotions. Defending territory calls for males to display their most brilliant colors from the most visible platforms. Yemen veiled chameleons, for instance, ascend to the tips of the highest branches in tamarind trees, assume their most brilliantly contrasting hues of gold and turquoise, and visibly dare another of their own sex and species to approach.

Sexual interest: The displays serve a second purpose as well—that of advertising a virile and successful male to any females within eyeshot. However, it is not only the males that use color and pattern to advertise sexuality—and other moods. The colors and patterns of the females are also indicators. One color advertises sexual nonreceptivity. Another advertises receptivity, and yet another says "I've been bred, I'm gravid; go away!"

Gravid Female Coloration

Panthers: Female panther chameleons, *Furcifer pardalis*, of *most* populations, are a rather unspectacular brownish-gray or brownish-green color when not gravid. Egg-carrying females intensify in color soon after breeding and within a week or two have assumed a deep brown coloration highlighted by large, light dorsolateral "portholes." As the deposition date nears, the portholes change to intense fiery orange.

Some of the most spectacular of all female color changes occur in a few of the more seldom seen Madagascar chameleons. It is the males of carpet, LaBord's, and the lesser chameleons that are the more subtly colored.

Carpets: The normally pale female carpet chameleon, *Furcifer lateralis*, assumes a pattern so complex when gravid that it beggars description. The highlights are yellow and rose suffused over straw and brown.

LaBord's: When gravid, the rather dull female LaBord's chameleon, *F. labordi,* assumes a lilac hue laterally, brilliant orange spots dorsally, and has a black-rimmed brilliant vermilion spot on each side of her neck. However, if not sexually receptive when approached by an amorous suitor, the female LaBord's chameleon becomes nearly jet black with small bright-blue dots.

Lesser: The even more seldom-seen lesser chameleon, *F. minor*, assumes a ground color of blackish-green when egg-laden. However, she also develops broad vertical bands of intense yellow, turquoise lateral spots, and the crown of her head turns vermilion—all this on a chameleon barely 6 inches in overall length!

The advertisement colors are truly of importance in these slow-moving, visually oriented, arboreal creatures. You need only to observe the interactions of several chameleons for a short time to determine exactly how important the colors are.

Dominant chameleons are brilliantly colored. Subordinate ones are dull to the point of obscurity. Nongravid females show enticement—or if not enticement, at least receptive—colors.

Clad in display colors, an adult male Chamaeleo c. calyptratus *views the world.*

Egg-laden females advertise their non-receptivity with screaming gaudiness.

It is little wonder that chameleons are creatures of intrigue to so many hobbyists and researchers! What is important is that the messages of color be correctly understood and interpreted.

Reproduction: Beyond Color

Cycling

Although many people consider merely keeping a chameleon hale and hearty a sufficient challenge, many of us wish to breed our lizards. While it is not easy, if compatible chameleons are kept in large enough facilities and are properly "cycled," successfully completing this objective is far from impossible. The term "cycled," as used here, pertains to the preparations—climatic, light duration, and others—that you should use to ready your chameleons for breeding.

External stimuli: The breeding sequences of most reptiles and amphibians are at least partially triggered by external stimuli. Among these stimuli, seasonal temperature changes, seasonal humidity changes, and photoperiods are prominent. Indeed, certain temperate-climate reptiles cannot be successfully bred unless they are subjected to a period of chilling and darkness similar to that which occurs during their periods of brumation (hibernation). Many chameleons are tropical creatures that do not undergo extended periods of dormancy; those species in Europe and the higher mountainous regions of Africa and Madagascar are the exception. But all areas experience certain annual climatic changes. These seasonal changes include reduced hours of daylight, lowered nighttime temperatures, reduced relative humidity, and a lessening of rain activity. The climatic changes are less

The vermilion dot on the side of the neck is characteristic of female LaBord's chameleons.

in the more tropical areas, being largely limited to a reduction of humidity and shower activity during the winter months.

Internal reactions: Slight though these changes may be, they play a profound role in the life cycle of the chameleon. During the periods of reduced light, temperature, humidity, and rainfall, reduction of the production of certain key hormones in the chameleon causes ovarian and testicular regression. With the lengthening days and corresponding increase in warmth, humidity, and rain activity, hormonal production once again increases, causing the changes that stimulate interest in reproduction. With the increase in the production of testosterone also comes increased interest in territoriality, with a correspondingly increased aggressive attitude toward rival males. It is at this time that hostility toward other chameleons increases.

Courtship

The courtship of a female chameleon by a male is characterized by stylized body language (rather similar to that used in territoriality displays) and color displays. Adult males are considerably larger than adult females. The body language involves pushups, head bobs, and nods and repeated dewlap distensions. After a whirlwind courtship the male will mount the female, retaining position by grasping her nape with his jaws. The male will curve and angle his body around that of the female until their cloacae are juxtapositioned. When their bodies are correctly positioned, intromission is usually quickly accomplished and is accompanied by a varied series of movements, including a "shrugging" sequence. After breeding is completed, the chameleons again go their separate ways.

Breeding timing: In the wild, throughout the late winter and early spring months chameleons are opportunistic breeders. Being loners, when the paths of two receptive chameleons of the opposite sex cross during those months, more often than not they will breed. A successful breeding will result in eggs within eight weeks, or live young in several months.

Nesting

For an egg-laying species, site preparation is important. After choosing a suitable site, the female will use her forefeet to dig deeply into the earth. Loosened dirt and debris is removed with the rear feet. When finished, the hole will be big enough to completely hide the female while she is laying. Usually, several times during preparations, the female will reverse her head-down position and peer quizzically from the deepening depression, perhaps scouting for approaching danger. Certainly during nest preparation she is more vulnerable to predation than at almost any other time in her life.

The nesting efforts may be curtailed at any time during the preparation. If disturbed by a predator or if the digging is thwarted by a maze of roots or rocks, the female will often leave to begin anew elsewhere at another time. Even if the nest is completed after several periods of digging interspersed with periods of rest, the female, based upon criteria known best to her, may deem the nesting chamber unsuitable. Should this be the case, the female will abandon the completed but unused nest and begin anew at another location and another time.

However, if all is deemed well with the initial excavation, the female will, after a period of rest, lay and position each egg of her clutch, then fill the hole with the removed dirt and leave. Depending on temperature and moisture, the period of incubation can and will vary considerably. At the low end,

under ideal nest conditions, the eggs may hatch in about six months. Under cooler, drier conditions, the incubation period may near a full 22 months.

Captive Breeding

Criteria for success: To breed your chameleons you (and they) need to meet several criteria. The most important of these, of course, is to have a sexual pair. Second, the pair needs to be temporarily compatible. Third, once successfully bred, the female needs to have a deposition chamber in which to lay her clutch, and fourth, you need the knowledge and facilities to hatch those viable eggs that are laid. Besides these basics, the use of several additional stimulatory cues may help you achieve your goal.

We will discuss two methods, one suitable to the benign climates of the lower Rio Grande Valley, southern Florida, and southern California where chameleons are often kept in outdoor settings, and a second method suitable for chameleons kept indoors in any climate.

We will assume that you do, in fact, have a pair of chameleons. "Tame," content, and healthy chameleons make the best breeders. If your chameleons are fearful and skittish, breeding sequences are easily interrupted.

Have your incubator set to proper humidity and temperature before actually having to use it. Remember that chameleon eggs literally like it cool.

Outdoors: Chameleons kept out of doors in the southernmost areas of our country can be allowed to breed and nest almost as they would in the wild. We, as owners, merely need to ascertain that suitable nesting areas are present in the cages. If the cage sits directly on the ground, the female will dig her nesting chamber into the ground.

Indoors: If the chameleon cage does not rest on the ground, or if your cage is indoors, you'll need to provide a large bucket of dampened sand as a nest-digging site.

Once the eggs have been laid, you'll need to remove and incubate them.

Some Hints for Inducing Reproduction

Although we now know more about the keeping and breeding of chameleons than ever before, there remains much more to learn. However, here are some pointers. Certain aspects may vary by species, or even populations (cool, high elevation versus warm, low elevation).

Cycling

As mentioned previously, the reproductive biology of even warm habitat chameleons is affected by the seasons. The term "seasons" may either indicate those that we in temperate climates consider normal (spring, summer, autumn, winter) or the less well-defined periods of rain versus the comparative dryness of the equatorial regions.

In either case, seasonal adjustments of temperature, humidity, and in some cases, photoperiod, have appeared effective in inducing spermatogenesis/ovulation in chameleons.

To cycle chameleons from north or south of the equator: Reduce normal daytime and nighttime temperatures by several degrees. Continue to provide a hotspot (warmed basking area) for a lesser number of hours daily.

Reduce food availability somewhat. This is especially important if your chameleons become largely quiescent. When food is offered, smaller meals of smaller than usual insects will be best.

Reduce relative humidity, actual dampness, and hours of illumination (photoperiod).

Continue this regimen for 60 to 90 days.

Chameleons from within a few degrees of the equator: Proceed as above, although a reduction of the photoperiod may not be as critical.

The reduction of both the relative and actual humidity factor is important. This can be accomplished by increasing the ventilation of the cage as well as reducing the amount of water used in everyday maintenance.

Increase to normal proportions after 60 to 90 days.

Live Bearers

Although the greatest number of chameleon species are oviparous (egg-layers), a fair number of species retain the eggs until they hatch internally, and so give birth to living young.

Live-bearers: Of these ovoviviparous species, it is the Jackson's chameleon, *Chamaeleo jacksonii* ssp., from Africa, that is most frequently seen in the United States. Other live-bearing forms are the little two-striped *C. bitaeniatus* and the high-casqued *C. hoehneli*, chameleons also of Africa. All South African members of the genus *Bradypodion*, often called dwarf chameleons, are ovoviviparous.

Several of these ovoviviparous chameleon species have been bred for many generations in captivity. European herpetoculturists have concentrated on the captive breeding of these interesting creatures.

Temperatures: It is particularly important that gravid female ovoviviparous chameleon species be provided a temperature regimen that is suitable for the development of the babies. Although the terrarium can be "cool" at night (temperatures of 65° to 72°F [18°–22°C]) with warmer day temperatures (74° to 80°F [23°–27°C]), a somewhat warmer basking spot will allow the female to increase her body temperature above that of the ambient should she choose. Overhead warmth-producing lighting (I use plant-growth bulbs) is best for this purpose when natural sunlight is not available.

Birth: The neonates are enclosed in a very thin membranous sac that adheres easily to most dry substrates. As the babies are expelled, the female chameleon often presses her vent against the branch or perch to which she is clinging. The enclosing sacs adhere to the branch and the babies will usually burst free with a few minutes time.

Females may also merely drop the babies on the substrate. It seems that the sudden stop galvanizes the babies to action and they immediately begin their efforts to escape. I have been told that a greater percentage of babies emerge from the dropped birthsacs than from the attached ones. Since contact with the air quickly dries and solidifies the sac, babies that don't emerge within the first few minutes will have an increasingly difficult time in emerging. If humidity is low, the sacs dry quite quickly. In the wild, babies that fail to emerge will die. In captivity, if you are present when the babies are born you can assist any of the weaker ones out of their sacs. Since these are almost always weak babies, they may not survive even with a human assist.

The young of these ovoviviparous species are usually born during the daylight hours. The ambient temperature may dictate to a degree when the females give birth. The females seem to choose the temperature at which the babies will be most active. It is possible that a cool temperature may inhibit the birthing event for a day or even more—until the return of suitable conditions.

Numbers: Some ovoviviparous chameleon species produce large litters of young. The clutches of a Jackson's chameleon can number from 10 to 50, in contrast to the 3 to 12 young per litter produced by many of the dwarf chameleons.

Egg Layers

Several weeks after successfully breeding, captive chameleons of oviparous (egg-laying) species will begin to seek a suitable egg-deposition site. If such a site is not regularly available within the cage, it must be provided. Most chameleons dig deep nests. This seems especially true of species from seasonally or perpetually arid habitats. In nature, deeper layers of the substrate better retain the moisture content necessary to prevent egg desiccation than shallower ones.

Even when captive, chameleons continue to dig deep nests. Female Yemen veiled chameleons that I have kept have repeatedly dug nests a full foot (30 cm) in depth, stopping only when they encountered the bottom of the nesting pail. A female common chameleon dug a nest 8 inches (20 cm) deep, and a female panther chameleon about 10 inches (25 cm). The shallowest nests were dug by a female carpet chameleon, who dug only 3 inches (7.5 cm) into the substrate, another of the same species who barely made a surface depression, and a female eyebrowed leaf chameleon who prepared no nest.

I have always allowed the female chameleons to complete the entire nesting sequence, from digging and readying the nest to laying and refilling the deposition burrow.

Female chameleons will advertise their readiness to lay. They will depart from their normal pattern of behavior by descending to the floor of the cage and wandering nervously about. It is at that time that I either place the nesting material in their cage or, if the weather is unsuitable (very cold or heavy rains), move the gravid female to an indoor nesting area. I do try to rush things along a little by keeping

A gravid female veiled chameleon digs her nest.

the nesting bucket brightly illuminated with an overhead bulb. When this is done, the female will continue to dig throughout the night. When the bucket is not lighted the female will often rest during most of the hours of darkness. The female is prevented from escaping by placing a covered wire-mesh sleeve around the bucket.

The entire nesting sequence can take up to 24 hours.

The nesting area is merely a 5-gallon pail filled to the brim with a suitably moistened sand/soil mixture. I mix it up well, adding just enough moisture to keep the nesting burrow from collapsing while the female is digging. If the soil is gently tamped after mixing and moistening, the walls of the nest burrow will have more structural integrity.

After the female has completed the nesting sequence and left the site, I carefully dig up and remove the eggs to a more controllable area for incubation.

HOW-TO:
Incubating Eggs

Making Your Own Incubator
You'll need:
- A heat tape
- A wafer thermostat (available at feed stores)
- A thermometer
- A styrofoam cooler with thick sides (a fish shipping box is ideal)

Poke a hole through the lid of the styrofoam cooler and suspend the thermostat/heater from the inside. Attach the contact wires of the heat tape to the thermostat. Add another hole in the styrofoam lid for a thermometer, so you can check on the inside temperature without opening the top. If there's no flange on the thermometer to

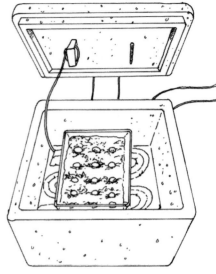

Inside view of incubator, showing thermostat and heat tape. The shoebox holding the eggs rests atop a "rack" of hardware cloth. The incubation medium consists of vermiculite, spagnum moss, or a mixture of peat and soil.

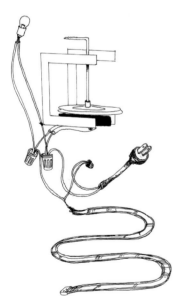

Use a wafer thermostat and a heat tape to make your own incubator.

keep it from slipping through the hole in the lid, use a rubber band wound several times around the thermometer to form a flange.

Put the lid on the cooler, and plug in the thermostat/heater. Wait half an hour and check the temperature. Adjust the thermostat/heater until the temperature inside the incubator is suitable and remains steady.

Removing the Eggs
When your chameleon has laid its eggs, remove them from the nest as soon as possible. When you do move the eggs, make sure you do not turn them. Keep the same side upward at all times. With reptile eggs, the position of the air pocket inside the egg should not change once the egg has been laid. If the egg is rolled over, the air pocket is moved and the embryo suffocates.

The eggs of chameleons are soft-shelled and permeable.

They are capable of both desiccating and overhydrating. Therefore, incubation conditions need to be fairly precise. Place the eggs in a series of containers, which in turn will be placed inside the incubator. Incubation is a simple but exacting process that involves keeping the eggs at the proper warmth and humidity.

The Incubation Medium
Vermiculite, sphagnum moss, or a mixture of equal parts of peat and soil make good incubation media. The vermiculite should be moistened with four parts of water to six parts of vermiculite, by weight. After it is thoroughly mixed, the eggs may be placed directly on, or half buried in, the dampened vermiculite. A shallow open dish of water in the incubator will help keep the relative humidity at 100 percent. If sphagnum or the peat and soil mixture is used, it should be thoroughly moistened, then squeezed as dry as

possible by hand. The eggs can be nestled in the moss. If the moss or vermiculite is too dry or too wet, the eggs will desiccate or overhydrate respectively. Both conditions can be fatal to developing embryos.

I prefer to keep each egg separated from its nearest neighbor by about an inch (2.5 cm). If the eggs are in contact with one another, the entire clutch, including those still slightly premature, may hatch simultaneously. Well-separated eggs are not apt to do this, hatching instead when development is complete.

Most feed stores sell styrofoam hen's egg incubators that are suitable for the incubation of chameleon eggs.

Controlling temperature and humidity. You'll need to monitor both the temperature and the humidity. The preferred humidity is 90 to 100 percent. This can be accomplished by keeping the hatching medium damp to the touch but too dry to squeeze out any water when squeezed by your hand. The normal temperature range of chameleon eggs varies by species. Check the species

A baby chameleon may be in no hurry to emerge from the egg.

accounts for the suggested temperature. Chameleon eggs are quite unlike the eggs of most other lizards in incubation durations. Some may take over 15 months to hatch and these may require a diapause (a cooling period when embryo development is slowed or halted).

Once you have the temperature regulated, place the containers of eggs inside the incubator and close the lid. Check the temperature daily and add a little water to the incubating medium as needed. You'll need to remove those

eggs with obvious problems, like fuzzy mold, but since the eggs aren't touching each other, the other eggs may not be spoiled.

If the eggs are infertile they may show obvious signs of spoiling in from one to several weeks. As mentioned above, discard spoiled eggs. Those that are fertile will remain white and turgid to the touch. Infertile eggs should be removed and discarded.

Hatching: Even after slitting (pipping) their eggs in preparation for emergence, the babies are really in no hurry to leave the egg. They may look out, and decide to stay inside the egg for a while longer, perhaps as long as a day and a half. Eventually, each egg that has matured enough to hatch, will. The live babies will emerge from the eggs and can be removed to another terrarium. Although they may not feed immediately, small insects can be offered. A sunning spot may or may not be used. Water should be provided by misting or a drip system.

(If any eggs remain unpipped, continue to incubate them until they go bad.)

A baby veiled chameleon emerging from its egg.

The Incubation Process

The egg clutches can vary from 1 or 2 with the smallest of the leaf chameleons to more than 80 with the Yemenese veiled chameleon.

Incubation temperatures vary tremendously but are always cooler than what you would inherently feel was good for them. The eggs of some of the montane species incubate well at 63° to 68°F (17–20°C). The eggs of some of the lowland and desert forms will withstand temperatures of 80° to 82°F (27–29°C). To determine what temperatures should be used, it is important that you know not only the exact species of chameleon with which you are working, but if it is a species that ranges widely in altitude (hence temperature ranges), you must know from where in its range the specimen came.

The eggs of many of the chameleons that incubate at cool temperatures seem to include a diapause (a temperature cessation of development) in their incubation cycle. The diapause often occurs during the driest or coolest part of the cycle. It may be necessary to simulate the diapause when eggs are being artificially incubated.

Eggs of most lowland/desert chameleons that normally incubate at fairly warm temperatures are not subject to a diapause.

If you are unsure of the temperature at which to incubate your chameleon's eggs, *err on the side of coolness.*

Why is the incubation duration so lengthy? Chameleons have adapted to some of the more inhospitable microhabitats within the tropics and subtropics of the Old World. Their activity patterns are often slowed or even halted by periods of drought or cold. In montane areas—even in the tropics—the cold can last for several weeks. There are some areas where soil temperatures never reach 70°F (21°C).

Many chameleon eggs laid at the beginning of good weather develop quickly for the few weeks of good weather, then enter a diapause which is brought about by cooling or drying soil conditions. The embryonic development largely stops for what may be a lengthy period. Continued development is brought about by a warming or rehydrating of the soil.

By the time embryonic development is complete, the tiny seasonal insects that will be so badly needed to fuel the rapid growth so typical of hatchling chameleons are again abundant.

Incubation and Sexual Maturity

Baby chameleons do grow quickly. It is possible for them to attain sexual maturity in less time than it took them to hatch.

Selected species	Incubation duration (in months)	Time to attain sexual maturity (in months)
Calumma brevicornis	6	8
Chamaeleo calyptratus	7–8	6
Furcifer campani	9	3–4
Chamaeleo chamaeleon	10	8
Chamaeleo gracilis	6–7	5–6
Furcifer lateralis	6–7	3
Chamaeleo montium	5–7	4–5
Furcifer pardalis	6–7	5–7
Calumma parsonii	16–22	9–12

Note: In each of the species accounts I have included suggested incubation temperatures. The eggs of most species that incubate for more than six months experience a diapause. With some species the optimum temperature and humidity during diapause remains unknown. Please record your successes and failures and make the information available to other hobbyists; chameleon-interest groups and publications are listed in Useful Literature and Addresses, page 99.

But a few days old, a neonate C. j. xantholophus *peers at the world. The rather large horn nubbins indicate this is a male.*

An Asocial African Beauty: The Veiled Chameleon

Range

The veiled chameleon, *Chamaeleo calyptratus*, comes from the mountainous desert areas of Yemen and Saudi Arabia. It can be found on the western slopes of a mountain range that begins in Yemen and ends in Saudi Arabia, and on the southern slopes of mountains on the tip of Yemen, at the entrance of the Red Sea. Those who keep *calyptratus* agree on two things: *calyptratus* is unique for its beauty, and among the asocial chameleons, this lizard is legendary for its extreme territoriality and aggressive behavior toward its own kind.

Appearance

The high hood (or casque) of a male of the nominate subspecies, measured from the corner of the mouth to the peak, may range from 3 to 4 inches (8–10 cm) in height. This is a truly impressive adornment. The female's casque is much lower.

It appears that the casque has several functions. Among others it increases the size of the lizard, and so makes it less attractive to potential predators, and it functions as a water condensation site, with the movable occipital flaps channeling the water to the corners of the mouth. This passive form of water "acquisition" works well in mountainous desert areas, where the night to day temperature fluctuations result in early morning dew condensation upon cooler surfaces.

In the early morning hours, the chameleons methodically seek out the warmest basking sites among the branches and turn themselves broadside to the sun. The side facing the sun will darken, increasing the amount of warmth absorbed. As the lizards warm, they become more active, and they begin to look around them. The coloration of the females, which darkens at night, pales to a light green with white or pale yellow spots and vertical streaks. The males also change their coloration. They brighten from their sleeping colors of dull slate or olive yellow to a brilliant series of dark-edged vertical turquoise and bright-yellow bars. The term "gaudy" is apt.

Sexual dimorphism: Males and females are sexually dimorphic, differing not only in coloration but in size as well. Overall length for the largest males is nearly 2 feet (60 cm), including the tail. Females are much smaller, attaining a length of about 14 inches (35 cm). Both sexes grow rapidly.

Males have tarsal (heel) spurs; females do not. The function of the spurs is unknown. The spurs are evident even on day-old male babies.

Captive Care

Remember that male *calyptratus* are usually aggressive lizards. Some can be unduly aggressive even toward females they are trying to mate. At times this can result in injuries to the female. Watch your lizards until you are certain that all is well. Aggressive behavior is more apt to manifest itself if the lizards are kept in small cages, or, if in large cages, where there are too few visual barriers. Adding visual barriers, no matter the size of the cage, may help stave off some savagery.

We kept a trio of *calyptratus* (one male and two females) together for several years. Their cage measured 4 × 2.5 × 6 feet (121 × 76 × 80 cm) and contained the usual crisscross of branches provided by a potted *Ficus* tree. Despite the fact that the male was one of the largest specimens I've ever seen and the females were small to average in size, no problematic interactions ever occurred. Both females produced several clutches of eggs throughout the warmer months of each year.

My tip: Many chameleons prefer coolness (not cold) over excessively warm conditions. To learn the temperatures at which your chameleons are more comfortable, read the appropriate species account. I have been unable to cover the needs of all 100-plus species of chameleons here, but in many cases it will be possible for you to extrapolate. Research both the range and the habitat of your species. If it is a montane form (one that prefers cool, moist highlands) opt for cagings such as shown for the little jeweled or the big Jackson's chameleons. If it is a hot lowland form, provide the caging suggested for the veiled or the graceful chameleons. If you are totally unsure, opt toward the cooler conditions but provide a warmed basking area. In other words, provide a thermal gradient. Allow the terrarium temperature to drop to between 65° and 68°F at night (18°–20°C) and raise it to 72° to 78°F (22°–26°C) in the daytime. The warmed basking area should enable

the chameleon to elevate its body temperature to 86° to 90°F (29°–33°C) if it chooses. Few will.

The road to keeping chameleons successfully can be plagued with detours of many kinds. Intelligent extrapolation will help ease your journey.

Diet

A diet of well-fed vitamin-dusted crickets, giant mealworms, nonnoxious grasshoppers (no lubbers, please), and waxworms will keep your *calyptratus* healthy. Please note: You need to feed gut-loaded crickets (see pages 28–29). My *calyptratus* nibbled occasionally on the shrubbery and greens offered in the cage for other lizards; their diet may not be wholly animal protein as thought.

Breeding

Calyptratus, both male and female, signal their breeding receptivity via skin coloration and patterning. For instance, a female *calyptratus*, when relaxed and unthreatened, displays her passive coloration of pale green with rows of white patches and dots. When receptive to breeding, she usually (but not always) adds sky blue "flash" markings along the back, tail, and on the casque.

Courtship: When you wish to breed your chameleons, if your male and female are not kept together as a matter of course, let the male and female see each other for a few minutes before you put them together.

If the female is not interested in breeding, her coloration will darken upon sight of the intended male. She will straighten her legs to stand erect, flatten her body, and warn him off with darkened coloration of dark green or black accented with bright blue and yellow spots. She will rock back on forth on her perch, expand her gular area, and glare at the male. If the male approaches too

In profile, it is easy to see the accentuated casque and gular crest of a male veiled chameleon, Chamaeleo c. calyptratus.

Orange and blue are incorporated into the colors of gravid female veiled chameleons.

closely, she will gape her mouth and exhale sharply.

The male *calyptratus* reacts to the sight of a female (or another male) with a typical male lizard territorial display. His colors brighten. He laterally flattens his body to appear larger, puffs out his throat area and nods his head. He approaches the female with a characteristic side-to-side swinging walk (almost a swagger), which helps show off his size and coloration. His tail will be tightly curled. It is at this stage that he is the most aggressive toward the female. He may bite and butt her repeatedly, hard enough to cause permanent damage. If this occurs, the two must be separated.

If the female finds the male attractive, she will keep her receptive coloration, turn, and slowly walk away. The male will follow, often butting her on the hips and tail region with his closed mouth. He will then mount her and juxtapose their vents. He will deposit sperm in her cloaca with one of his two hemipenes, and then dismount. The entire mating may take several minutes, and can be repeated several times in one day.

Gravid behavior: A female that has been impregnated will begin to reject all males anywhere from 18 hours to 3 days after the copulation. She will demonstrate this rejection by evoking her darkened warning coloration upon sighting another *calyptratus*, male or female. When left alone or unstressed, a gravid female may display her normal passive coloration or her receptive breeding coloration of green and white with blue flashings.

Gravid female *calyptratus* exhibit increased basking time just before egg deposition. Since the sun's UV rays (between the wavelengths of 290 to 315 nanometers) are essential for the conversion of vitamin D_3, it seems that this increased basking time has a very real function.

Even after laying her eggs, the female usually will continue to display warning coloration to any male encountered for several weeks following egg deposition. After that she may display her receptive coloration, although she does not need to mate again to lay her next clutch of fertile eggs.

Eggs

Chamaeleo calyptratus is a fecund species. Captive females first become receptive to mating for a period of 10 to 15 days at the very young age of 3½ to 5 months of age. They are again receptive to mating about 60 days after egg deposition. Captive females that are not bred during that first receptive period almost always die egg-bound when they do become gravid.

The females can lay multiple clutches after a single sperm deposition, and may need to breed only once. Females lay clutches of 27 to 80 eggs, from 3 to 4 times a year, with the larger females laying the larger clutches. This type of deposition seriously depletes the strength of the female. Captive females rarely live beyond their fifth or sixth clutch.

In contrast, *calyptratus* in the wild lay far fewer eggs, from 12 to 20. It is not known specifically what regulates the clutch size, whether it is seasonal or daily temperature fluctuation, changed nutritional levels, or some other unidentified factor, nor do we know how long the females live in the wild.

Other Subspecies

The second subspecies of the veiled chameleon, *C. c. calcarifer*, has a much lower head casque. They are also somewhat smaller and much less frequently seen as captives.

A head-on view of a hatchling veiled chameleon.

Chamaeleo calyptratus calcarifer *is a smaller, less well adorned subspecies of the veiled chameleon.*

49

A Showy *Furcifer:* The Panther Chameleon

Range

A denizen of varied habitats, the panther chameleon, *Furcifer pardalis*, occurs along the northwestern, northern, and east coast of mainland Madagascar. It also occurs on many coastal islands. It is found from sea level to elevations of 4,000 feet (1,230 m), and from scrublands to open secondary forest. Temperature within its range varies from the high nineties Fahrenheit (36°C) on summer days to 35°F (2°C) on winter nights.

Pardalis is most common in warm, humid climates with a moderate seasonal fluctuation. They do not like deeply shaded forest habitat, and are what we would term a "forest-edge" species, preferring the forest where it borders agricultural habitat.

Appearance: The species is sexually dimorphic, with the males reaching a total length of 22 inches (56 cm) and the females reaching 13 inches (33 cm). Males have a small, vaguely forked rostral projection and are known for spectacular color variations among populations. The colors are most intense during breeding season. Most males have varying amounts of red or orange on the face, legs, and tail, but the color variations get wilder from there.

Males from Nosy Be, a small island off the northwestern tip of Madagascar, are uniform light blue-green to turquoise with a light to white side stripe. Their lips are bright yellow. Other males from Nosy Be are uniformly turquoise, and are called, with an odd sort of logic, "blue phase." Body bars on these are usually faint or absent.

Males from Ambanja, a coastal town just across the waterway from Nosy Be, are light blue-green with bright burgundy or red vertical body bars, highlighted with the horizontal light stripe on each side. The lips are light-colored. During social displays, the eye turrets of these males flush with patterns of red, yellow, or green.

Males from Diego Suarez, at the far northern tip of Madagascar, resemble the males from Ambanja but can change their body color from green to yellow (the body bars and eye turrets of burgundy remain).

Males from the eastern coast of Madagascar, from the towns of Maroansetra to Tamatave, are usually dark green with either none or only vague body bars. The dorsal crest, the area along the backbone, is usually lighter and forms a gray stripe. The broken stripe along the side of the body is a pale fawn color, while the eye turrets color up during social display to a distinctive pattern of black and gray. Males from at least two of these eastern coastal populations can change their coloration from dark green to a uniform bright orange-red in a matter of seconds. The more brilliantly red specimens are from the towns of Sambava and Maroansetra on the northwestern tip of Madagascar.

Most females exhibit little change from population to population. Females are usually pale gray-green with vertical russet bands. One notable exception was a female owned by Bill Love. From northeastern Madagascar, this female's day-in, day-out coloration was brilliant orange with brown bands. A prominent white lateral stripe was present.

As a matter of fact, no matter what the color or pattern, both sexes invariably have a light, longitudinal, midlateral stripe on each side.

Diet

Pardalis eat a lot, almost the equivalent of their body mass per week in vitamin-dusted, gut-loaded (VDGL) crickets—this translates to the active consumption of 30 to 50 crickets a week—and other insects. As with other chameleons, panthers will tire of a diet that consists of the same type of insects day after day. Dietary variation is the keynote to success. Besides crickets, offer giant mealworms, butterworms, waxworms, field plankton, roaches, and if your specimens are particularly large, pinky mice. Some *pardalis* will also accept non-toxic blossoms such as dandelions, nasturtiums, and rose petals.

Breeding

Male *pardalis* are highly territorial during the breeding season. They team up with females only during the breeding season, preferring to remain well spaced in their habitat of low-growing trees and shrubs. Both sexes seem to prefer to stay six feet (1.8 m) or so off the ground, although they occasionally are found higher up.

Male to male reactions include a territorial display of lateral body compression, puffing out the gular area, tail coiling, and dramatic color changes of the eye turrets. The male seeking to dominate will move toward his rival. If the rival does not retreat, the challenger will begin the fight, which sometimes starts with a head butting contest and progresses to biting and lunging.

Courtship: As with other species of chameleons, if the male and female panther chameleon have not been kept together, it is best to let them see each other before placing them in the same enclosure for breeding. After a few minutes, the male will usually have cooled off enough (and the female have indicated interest, as demonstrated by her coloring) for courtship to proceed.

When the female *pardalis* is interested in breeding, she will exhibit her receptive coloration. Her body coloration will fade to an overall white or fawn, turning to pale pink on her underside. If she is not interested, she will darken in tone, her crossbars becoming more distinctive, gape her mouth, and turn so that her side view is visible to the male.

The male will indicate his interest by the increased brilliance of his body color and eye turret color, much the same changes as in male-to-male encounters, but his behavior will be far less aggressive. The male will bob his head, and approach the female.

If the female is receptive, she will keep her pale coloration. The male will mount her and twist so their vents are juxtaposed. Copulation may last from 10 to 30 minutes.

Gravid behavior: Once gravid, the female panther chameleon will display a new color pattern, one of overall earthen tones with a series of orange or tan "portholes" on each side. She will not be receptive to any males (although she will be receptive two to three weeks after egg deposition).

This specimen from northeastern Madagascar is the most brilliantly colored female panther chameleon, Furcifer pardalis, *I have yet seen.*

Gravid female panther chameleons assume a pattern of orange "portholes."

This spectacular male turquoise morph panther chameleon is from the island of Nosy Be.

Hatchling panther chameleons are dull but "cute." This specimen emerged from the egg with a damaged tail-tip.

Eggs

The female can produce several egg clutches a year, with 12 to 50 eggs per clutch. Incubation takes from 6 to 12 months, and at least in the wild, appears to be timed so the young emerge during the warm season. Those young that survive until the next warm season are sexually mature and begin breeding. There is a high mortality among egg-laying females, and it appears that few of them survive beyond the second year, either in the wild or in captivity.

The gravid female needs to be isolated and provided with an egg-laying area three to six weeks after breeding. She will dig a tunnel in a container of moistened sand or potting soil, lay her eggs and fill the tunnel with the loosened soil. As soon as she has completed tamping down the dirt in the tunnel, offer her food and water.

When incubated at 73° to 76°F (22°–25°C) the eggs hatch in about five and a half months.

Note: Of the many chameleon species available, *F. pardalis* is one of the most desirable from the herpeToculturist's viewpoint. They are beautiful, variable, hardy, and prolific. There could hardly be a better set of characteristics.

Some Miniature Triceratops: Three-horned Chameleons from Africa

The Poroto Moutain Three-horned Chameleon

Range

Chameleo fuelleborni is a species that is rather poorly known in herpeto-cultural circles. It is only little better known in nature. It is apparently restricted in distribution to the Ngosi Volcano in Tanzania's Poroto Mountains. It is known to be ovovivip-arous, but clutch size and gestation parameters are unknown. It is thought that since it is a forest species of mod-erate to high elevations, it would do best at cool temperatures.

The few specimens that I have seen since the initial imports have not given me the impression of being particularly delicate. As a matter of fact, those that I watched at Glades Herp ate well and drank readily until they were sold. I rather think that the species would do well if offered the same regimen of care that will be discussed here for the Jackson's chameleon.

Appearance

The Poroto Mountain three-horned chameleon would appear to be a small species. The males I have seen were in the 7- to 8-inch-long (18–20 cm) range and the females were slightly smaller.

Johnston's Chameleon

Johnston's vs. Jackson's: In direct contrast to the poorly known *C. fuelleborni*, both the Johnston's and the Jackson's chameleon are well known and often bred. Of these two it is Jackson's chameleon which is the most in demand and Johnston's which is less expensive. The Johnston's chameleon has proven more delicate than the Jackson's.

Range

The various subspecies of *C. johnstoni* (three by the reckonings of some authorities, two by others) occur in equatorial central Africa. There they may be found in habitats as diverse as savannas and cloud forests, at altitudes between 3,100 and 8,400 feet (950–2,600 m). The habitats are damp and well-watered and average between 55°F on the coolest nights to nearly 85°F on the warmest days (13°–29°C). Although there is not a lot of rain (40 to 65 inches; 100–165 cm annually), nei-ther is there a well-pronounced dry season. The damp warmth allows *C. johnstoni* to be active year around.

Appearance

Chamaeleo johnstoni is a species of variable appearance. When most people think of the species, they visualize *C. j. johnstoni*, a pretty little (actually, moderately sized) chameleon, the males with a trio of long, annulated horns. The pair of pre-orbital horns often curve gently downward; the rostral horn may curve very gently upward. Females lack horns. But both sexes lack horns in another subspecies of *johnstoni*, *C. j. ituriensis*, which is less frequently seen in the pet trade. The few hobbyists who have seen the third form, *C. j. ituriensis*, find them attractive but, when compared to the nominate form, of unexciting appearance.

Healthy, nonstressed male *C. j. johnstoni* are pretty animals. Typically, the ground color of a contented male is a bright and attractive bluish-green. Four broad, irregularly edged dark bands are often visible with variably placed blue patches, and dark flecks are present. Yellow areas may occur dorsolaterally in the green areas. Males occasionally exceed a foot (31 cm) in total length. The females are somewhat smaller. Most females measure between 9 and 11 inches (12–28 cm) in total length. Sexually receptive females are a more or less vaguely patterned (almost unicolor) bluish-green. The dark bandings, when present, are most prominent dorsally. The sides of her head often bear turquoise and peach markings. Nonreceptive females are much more strongly banded and brightly colored and the peach markings on the face may brighten to a rather brilliant orange.

Captive Care

Johnston's chameleon is a rather hardy chameleon that adapts well in captivity to life in "family" groups. Single males have lived harmoniously with from three to five females in my step-in cages for rather long durations. Males are incompatible with others of their sex and will joust with their horns or actually savagely bite each other.

Breeding

Johnston's chameleon is the only one of the triceratops-lookalikes to be oviparous. Females dig rather deep nesting chambers, and when captive, prefer a more easily worked, yielding loam substrate to sand.

Eggs

The eggs number between 5 and 23, with smaller females producing fewer eggs. Females become sexually mature at between four and five months of age. The incubation duration is rather short for a moderately sized chameleon species. At a temperature of from 72° to 76°F (22°–25°C), hatching can occur in about three and a half months.

Caution: Although Johnston's chameleons are considered a rather hardy species, they are prone to one very disconcerting malady: edema. This not only produces unsightly swellings in the gular and anterior thoracic regions, but is considered symptomatic of organ dysfunction. Many herpetoculturists feel that hypervitaminosis (the overmetabolizing of an excess of vitamins) is the underlying cause and that vitamin A, in particular, is the main culprit.

Vitamin A may or may not be the cause of edema, but because an excess of this vitamin has been linked to liver damage, it seems prudent to limit—not eliminate—its intake.

Jackson's Chameleons

As with other chameleons, the common name actually refers to several subspecies. With the group known as "the Jackson's," there are three subspecies. Two of the three races are rather readily available commercially.

The Meru Mountains Jackson's chameleon, *C. j. merumontana*, is a smaller race and the least common of the three in American herpetoculture. It commands both common and scientific names from the Tanzanian mountain range to which it is endemic. Both males and females have preorbital and rostral processes.

The nominate race, *C. j. jacksonii*, is the more common of the two smaller forms. Males attain a length of about 10 inches (25 cm); females are somewhat smaller. The males are typically triceratops-like in appearance; the females usually have a rostral process (obscure to prominent) but lack the preorbital processes. This race occurs widely in Kenya and Tanzania, but is absent from the Arusha district of the Meru Mountains of Tanzania and the southern slopes of Mt. Kenya, Kenya. In the former it is replaced by the previously mentioned *C. j. merumontana* and in the latter by the larger and beautiful *C. j. xantholophus*.

Mt. Kenyan: When hobbyists mention *Chamaeleo jacksonii* (or simply "Jackson's chameleon") without designating a subspecies, it is usually the beautiful Mt. Kenyan *C. j. xantholophus* about which they are speaking. It is the largest subspecies and the one most frequently available to herpetoculturists. The males of this form can reach slightly over 13 inches (33 cm) in total length and the females are only slightly smaller. The females lack both preorbital and rostral processes.

Range

In the 1960s and 1970s a great many Jackson's chameleons were imported for the American pet trade from the east African country of Kenya. However, from those early years until 1993 very few wild-collected Jackson's chameleons were seen on the American market. Those that were available to hobbyists were captive-bred and -born babies that always commanded rather high prices. In 1993 (up to today, 1995) a few wild-collected Mt. Kenyan Jackson's chameleons again became available—these were from Hawaii, where the species has been known to exist in the wild, established breeding colonies since 1972. A fair-sized breeding colony was also known to exist in Hillsborough County, Florida, from the mid-sixties to the early seventies. After that time I lost contact with the owners of the land on which the chameleon colony was located and no longer know whether it continues to exist.

Appearance

Although capable of considerable color changes, the Mt. Kenyan Jackson's chameleon is usually of some shade of green. This may vary from almost black if the animals are severely stressed to a basically unpatterned lime green when they are courting. A bright green appears if the males are involved in territorial displays. An overall light green is assumed when sleeping. A rather deep olive with darker banding or irregular flecking is not uncommon when they are content. A deep olive brown is also a regularly seen color. Complex lichenate colors and patterns are frequently assumed. A thin to thick light dorsolateral line, either entire or broken into dashes, may or may not be present. In other words, variability is the name of the game with the juveniles and adults of this wonderful lizard. The neonates are most often tan or very light gray.

Captive Care

As with most chameleons, more than a single male cannot be kept to a cage. However, family groupings of one male and one to four females can be kept if the cage is large enough. When I lived in southern Florida I found this species did well outside during our winters, but languished

The horns of the adult female Poroto Mountain chameleon, C. fuelleborni *(left) are smaller than those of the male (right).*

Many female Johnston's chameleons Chamaeleon johnstoni, *have orange on the snout.*

Although rather inexpensive, adult male Johnston's chameleons are of impressive appearance.

Note the single horn borne by this female Chamaeleo j. merumontanus.

This pretty specimen is a male Chamaeleo jacksonii merumontanus.

during the summer's heat. In the United States, the greatest success this species has had in captivity has been achieved in coastal southern California. There they can be kept outdoors year round. This is a temperature-tolerant species that would prefer daytime highs in the 74° to 84°F (23°–28°C) range with drops at night to 50° to 64°F (10°–17°C). They can withstand temperatures much cooler than this (even sustaining freezing temperatures for very short periods) but dislike warmer temperatures.

Diet

Roaches, giant mealworms, butterworms, crickets, and other similar sized insects are consumed by adult Jackson's chameleons. Caterpillars, snails, and other such wild-collected fare can be offered from insecticide-free areas.

If they are given ample diets, suitable space, and plenty of water, I suspect that you will find Jackson's chameleons one of the more rewarding species with which to work. Although this species does not seem prone to any particular ailments (including the edema that often plagues the look-alike Johnston's chameleon), keeping them clean and their quarters well-ventilated will help stave off potential problems.

Breeding

Male Jackson's chameleons (of all three races) are very territorial; females are less so. It has been ascertained that a single male may stake out a very large tree or an equally large patch of shrubs as its individual territory. "Turf" is defended against other males by display (posturing and color changes), jousting (horn to horn combat), or actual biting.

Jacksons chameleons are ovoviviparous. Clutches may number from 8 to 50 babies (usually 15 to 25) that are

Female Chamaeleo jacksonii xantholophus *lack horns.*

born enclosed in sticky, membranous sacs. The sacs readily adhere to branches and leaves, but may also be merely dropped to the ground. The neonates tear themselves free from their birth sacs soon (usually within 10 minutes) after being expelled by the female. If the relative humidity is low, the birth sacs may dry very quickly and it becomes difficult for the babies to free themselves. Under such conditions a human assist may be necessary. If relative humidity is normally high, it is only the weakest babies that fail to emerge from the sacs. These weakest babies may die even if given a human assist. Babies are more adversely affected by very low temperatures than the females. Keep nighttime lows above 68°F (20°C) for the first few weeks of their lives. Two clutches may be produced annually by adult females.

Longevity: These are fairly long-lived chameleons. Under suitable conditions a lifespan of a decade may be attained.

Four Small *Furcifers*: LaBord's, Lesser, Petter's, and Will's Chameleons

There are three small chameleons in Madagascar of which the females are prettier and more complexly colored than the males at any time, and which are absolutely magnificent when gravid. All are members of the genus *Furcifer* (the genus *Furcifer*, by the way, is divided into several complexes which are definable externally by the presence or lack of a nasal structure.) None of these three, LaBord's, *F. labordi*; the lesser, *F. minor*; and Will's, *F. willsii*, chameleons are particularly common in the United States, but all are imported regularly in small numbers. A fourth *Furcifer*, Petter's chameleon, *F. petteri*, although no less interesting, is somewhat less colorful and even less frequently imported than the others.

The small sizes of these four chameleons makes them ideal candidates for rather small but well-ventilated and cool facilities. A daytime high of 72° to 76°F (22°–25°C) is adequate for all, but a warmer basking area should also be provided. Gravid females seem to bask with slightly greater frequency than nongravid females or males. Nighttime lows of 60° to 65°F (16°–18°C) are not harmful for adults, but herpetoculturists who have hatched the babies of some of these forms advise a low of 70°F

(21°C) for the hatchlings. Nighttime cage temperatures for gravid females should not drop lower than the high sixties (19°–21°C).

The nose tells: The lesser, Will's, and Petter's chameleons are in the *F. bifidus* complex. The male members of this group have paired, bony nasal adornments, while the females lack these structures.

LaBord's chameleon is in the *F. rhinoceratus* complex, the members of which are defined by having a single, paddlelike nasal structure, largest on males, but not entirely lacking on females.

LaBord's Chameleon

Range

This interesting little chameleon dwells in trees and shrubs in the forested lowlands of central western Madagascar. Of the three species mentioned in this section, *labordi* is the most tolerant of warmth.

Appearance

The very largest of the males of LaBord's chameleon may measure close to, but rarely exceed, a length of 12 inches (30 cm). The females seldom exceed 6.5 inches (17 cm). Males have a well-developed casque, but are not colorful. They are generally of some shade of green, gray-green, or greenish-brown, usually at least vaguely banded, and have a prominent light midlateral stripe. The males also have a rather prominent serrate vertebral "crest." The females are very much more colorful. When undisturbed, nongravid females are predominantly green laterally, but have irregular series of mauve spots and streaks. Brilliant orange spots are present on either side of the vertebral ridge. The top of the head is often predominantly orange. A brilliant red spot is present on each side of the neck.

When the females are gravid, the blue spots expand, often suffusing at least 50 percent of the sides with a color that varies from mauve to violet. The remaining areas of the sides are black (or blackish). A gravid female who is approached by a male often becomes almost entirely black. In both cases the orange paravertebral spots are retained.

Eggs

The egg clutches are small, usually consisting of 6 to 15 eggs. Several clutches can be produced in a season. The suggested incubation for this species is in the 75° to 78°F (24°–26°C) range and the eggs will require an incubation duration of about seven and a half months. If fed heavily on vitamin/mineral-enhanced insects, the babies will grow quickly. They will attain sexual maturity in about four months' time but will continue to grow for a period well beyond that.

The Lesser Chameleon

The lesser chameleon, F. minor, is one of my favorites. It is small, the females are exquisitely beautiful (the males much less so), and it appears to be quite hardy.

Range

Found at moderate elevations along the southeastern slopes of the central Madagascar plateau, F. minor is a species well adapted to cooler temperatures. In fact, F. minor will languish if forced to endure the hot summer temperatures of our southern tier states.

Appearance

The 9-inch (22-cm) long males of F. minor are usually broadly banded with tan (or pinkish-tan) on brown. Occasional specimens may be quite dark. The nasal protuberances are prominent and it has a weak vertebral crest. Two dark-edged light spots are present anteriolaterally. Although young, nongravid females may be quite plainly colored in light green, gravid females are truly eye-catching. Most are clad in broad, alternating bands of black and intense yellow. There are tiny yellow dots scattered over the black areas. Two turquoise to violet spots are present anterio-laterally. And to top all of this off, the crown of the head, and occasionally the sides of the lower jaw, are clad in scales of intense vermilion. Females are adult at about 5½ inches (13 cm) in length.

Eggs

In keeping with its small size, F. minor has rather small egg clutches. From 4 to 15 eggs (usually 10 to 12) are normally laid. A single healthy female can lay several clutches a season. The incubation period is about eight months at a temperature of 69° to 70°F (20°–21°C). The hatchlings are only about 1¼ inches in length (3 cm). The hatchlings seem even hardier than the adults, feeding readily on all manner of tiny insects and arthropods. Growth is fast, and they reputedly attain sexual maturity in less than six months.

Although much duller than his mate, the male LaBord's chameleon, F. labordi, *has a paddle-like rostral process.*

Gravid female lesser chameleons, Furcifer minor, *are spectacularly colored.*

Male Furcifer minor *have prominent rostral appendages but lack brilliant colors.*

Petter's Chameleon

So similar is *F. petteri*, Petter's chameleon, to *F. willsii*, that it was thought for some time to be a sub-species of the latter. The nasal appendages of *F. petteri* are quite different than those of *F. willsii*, however. Those of *petteri* are broadly separated at the base and parallel each other, having no partial spiral. The nasal appendages of *F. willsii* have a partial spiral, not entirely parallel. Other anatomical differences have also been noted.

Range

Petter's chameleon is a species that is found on the extreme northern tip of Madagascar. Rather recently a specimen was found several hundred kilometers south and west. Whether the species exists in the remaining forests between is not known. At the moment, this remains a little-known chameleon.

Appearance

Both the male and female of *F. petteri* are green in color. Females of Petter's chameleons often (but seemingly not invariably) have two white spots on the forward part of each side. Males *may* have a white lateral stripe. Whether or not gravid females assume colors more brilliant than nongravid ones is not known. However, it would be rather expected that they do. Male *F. petteri* attain a length of approximately 6.5 inches (16 cm); fully grown females are generally an inch or two shorter (11–14 cm).

Will's Chameleon

Range

Will's chameleon is found in central eastern Madagascar. It seems to prefer higher altitudes and shuns excessive heat.

Appearance

Most external features of *F. willsii*—size, overall conformation, and color—are very similar to those mentioned for Petter's chameleon. The most striking difference is in the nasal appendages (mentioned in the section on Petter's). The lateral stripe of *F. willsii* often extends only on the anterior half of the sides. Although females do have two light anteriolateral spots, a pattern of light transverse stripes is usually also apparent (especially when the female is gravid). Gravid females also tend to have a darker ground color, this being blackish green or even charcoal-black.

Eggs

The reproductive biology of *F. willsii* is fairly well documented. The species can lay up to 15 eggs and may have up to 3 clutches during a single season. From 70° to 73°F (21°–23°C) seem to be satisfactory incubation temperatures. Incubation varies from five and a half to seven months. Hatchlings are a little over 1¼ inches (3 cm) in total length. Captive hatched babies have fine appetites and grow quickly.

Note: Most of these small chameleons either brumate or become dormant during the cooler months of the Madagascar winter. It is thought that this seasonal cycling contributes significantly to their fecundity. Certainly cooling, reduced humidity, and reduced hours of daylight are used extensively when breeding other forms of chameleons.

It is likely that as our expertise with these little creatures increases, we will find the answers to many of our current questions. If you do decide to work with any of these forms, we urge you to keep records and share your knowledge. Even adverse results can help others not to make the same mistake.

Petter's chameleons, F. petteri, *of both sexes are clad in scales of green. The female lacks the rostral adornment.*

Although certainly not brightly colored, gravid female Wills' chameleons, F. willsii, *are attractive.*

Males of Wills' chameleons, Furcifer willsii, *may be green or almost black.*

A Trio of Madagascan Beauties: The Carpet, Jeweled, and Elephant-eared Chameleons

When you begin looking at chameleons, you can't help but begin to rate them either by ease of keeping, size, or even as the prettiest. And when you're working with a group as colorful and as eye-catching as the chameleons, the accolade "prettiest" really means something. Let's take a look at three of the most beautiful small chameleons. They represent two genera, *Furcifer* and *Calumma*.

The first two, the carpet and the jeweled, form the lateralis group of the genus *Furcifer*. They are, respectively, *F. lateralis* and *F. campani*. They are common, rather delicate, extraordinarily beautiful, and very inexpensive.

The Carpet Chameleon

The carpet chameleon has derived its common name, not because it is continually underfoot or because it enters houses, but rather because the intricate pattern and brilliant colors of the gravid females remind one of the richness of an oriental carpet. Once you understand the etymology, the name seems appropriate enough, for these truly are a beautiful chameleon species.

Range

Carpet chameleons are dwellers of moderate altitudes, and do best at moderate temperatures. Specimens are widely distributed over most of Madagascar. Individuals are even a common sight on shrubs and bushes well within the limits of many cities— the capital included.

Appearance

There is no marked dissimilarity in size between the sexes of the carpet chameleon. Females tend to be of heavier build. Both attain a length of 7½ to 10 inches (17–25 cm).

Males of the carpet chameleon are green and have a thin, white mid-lateral line. Gravid females have a pattern of brown bands separated by cream or yellow, dark lateral ocelli (open-centered rings), often a poorly defined rich orange or orange-red mid-lateral stripe, a tan-peppered brown belly, and yellow-peppered brown legs. The throat and lips are spotted and striped, dark on light. The tail is barred for its entire length. Nongravid females lack the richness of color but are rather similarly marked. Neither sex has either nasal projection or occipital lobes (flaps).

As with many of the Madegascan chameleons, it is the gravid females of the carpet that are the most beautiful. They are also the most easily stressed by shipping, and since almost every female carpet chameleon received in the United States is gravid, it is small wonder that the mortality is high.

Captive Care

Well-ventilated terraria with a daytime high of 78° to 84°F (23°–28°C) need a slightly warmer basking area, especially for gravid females, and a nighttime low of 66° to 72°F (18°–22°C). Gravid females should not be subjected to temperatures below 70°F (21°C).

If carpet chameleons are healthy when received, they actually do quite well. However, most are debilitated to a greater or lesser degree. Newly received specimens should be checked immediately for endoparasites. As virtually all on the pet market are wild-collected and imported from Madagascar, most *will* be parasitized. Additionally, these chameleons are often dehydrated when received. Drinking water should be offered several times daily, either in a mist or drip form, until they are adequately rehydrated. They should not be subjected to excessive heat.

Eggs

Female carpet chameleons will lay several clutches of from 10 to 20 eggs annually. Incubation temperatures of 70° to 75°F (21°–24°C) seem best. At the high end of this range, incubation will take somewhat less than six months.

Longevity: Both the carpet and the jeweled chameleons seem to have very short lifespans in the wild. It is reported that most do not survive more than a year and a half. Carpet chameleons have been kept at least twice that time in captivity. We remain less successful with jeweled chameleons, though.

Note: A few very large (more than 12 inches or 30 cm), pretty, lime-green male carpet chameleons have been trickling in. These have been imported under the name of "giant carpet chameleon, *F. l. major.*" The females

that have been imported with them have been identical in all appearances to typical *lateralis*. The taxonomic name is actually of questionable validity.

The Jeweled Chameleon

The jeweled chameleon, *Furcifer campani*, is another species of remarkable beauty. While the pattern of this little (to 7 inches or 18 cm) chameleon is nearly as "busy" as that of the carpet chameleon, it is arranged very differently.

Strangely, although the males and females are similarly patterned and colored, it is mostly the gravid females of this species that are imported to the United States.

Range

F. campani is restricted in distribution to the highest elevations of the central Madagascar plateau and, apparently, brumates for a period of several weeks each winter. It is even reported in areas of considerable snowfall.

Appearance

The ground color of *F. campani* is usually a very pretty and rather bright green. Some specimens (especially those that are distressed) are quite dark and less pleasingly colored. Three light longitudinal lines are present on each side. These dorsolateral and lateral lines are butter yellow, ochre, or bright yellow. The third line, the ventrolateral line, is often (but not invariably) a lighter tan to white. Profusely scattered over the darker areas of the body are discrete yellow, reddish, or even turquoise dots. According to Rob Macinnes of Glades Reptiles, the body shape of the male is more lanceolate and a "huge" hemipenial bulge is present.

Captive Care

The jeweled chameleon is a rather difficult species to maintain success-

An angry elephant-eared chameleon, Calumma brevicornis, *displays.*

looking nearly identical, sibling species are usually genetically differentiated from each other and thus are incapable of interbreeding.

Range

As currently understood, the elephant-eared chameleon has a tremendous range. It occurs southward along the eastern slopes of the island from the northern tip of Madagascar to near Ihosy (three-quarters of the way southward along the east coast). It also occurs from the lowland forested areas to near the tops of the highest mountains.

Appearance

Long known as the "short-horned" chameleon, the new designation of "elephant-eared" chameleon seems at least as good if not better. When threatened, *brevicornis* actually is capable of raising its large elephant-earlike occipital flaps upward. This is an impressive display for this usually grayish 12- to 15-inch- (30–38 cm) long creature.

Most elephant-eared chameleons are subtly colored in shades of gray. Some have a russet to terracotta suffusion to the "ears" and body. Displaying males occasionally assume a greenish-gray (but *not* green) body color.

Sexual dimorphism: The females are slightly the smaller of the two sexes and lack the hemipenial bulges (bulges at the base of the tail) that are more or less noticeable on the males. The females have only vague indications of the rostral protrusion. All members of the complex have a continuous serrate vertebral crest and heavy tails which are often kept tightly coiled.

Captive Care

When purchasing specimens of *C. brevicornis* for potential breeding projects, it would be best to purchase

fully. The six to ten eggs are best incubated at temperatures in the mid-sixties F (63°–67°F or 17°–20°C). Incubation time is nearly 10 months. The very few young which have been hatched in the United States have been reported difficult to raise.

The Elephant-eared Chameleon

To begin with, the beautiful elephant-eared chameleons, *Calumma brevicornis*, are not common, not delicate, and (alas) not inexpensive. *Brevicornis* is also not a single species; it seems almost certain that we are dealing with a complex of sibling species rather than just a single, variable chameleon. These sibling species are part of the *cucullata* group of the genus *Calumma*, all from Madagascar.

The fact that we are dealing with a group of closely related chameleons might well account for the merely sporadic breeding success had with this species in the United States. Despite

The carpet chameleon, Furcifer lateralis, *takes its common name from the intricate pattern and colors of the gravid female.*

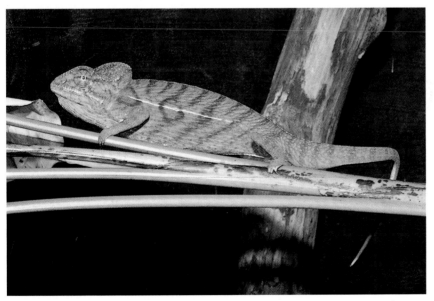

Male carpet chameleons from the extreme southwest of Madagascar are larger and more brightly colored than most other specimens. The name of F. l. major *is often used to designate them.*

all at the same time (perhaps this will enhance your chances of getting specimens collected in close proximity to one another) and to examine the creatures in question carefully. Choose those that are the most similar. For instance, choose all with either gray legs *or* blue legs—don't mix the two. Don't mix gray and green "*brevicornis*."

Look carefully at the occipital lobes (neck flaps). Ascertain that the central (vertebral) division of the flaps is exactly similar. Don't mix specimens with deep divisions with those with shallow or no divisions.

Check the comparative lengths of the short snout protrusion (from which the species takes its scientific designation). If there are some males with fairly long extensions, others with only moderate ones, and still others with no nose horn, the origins of the specimens were probably widespread. You may have difficulty getting reproductively compatible specimens from such a group (except by sheer accident).

Eggs

As with many chameleons, *brevicornis* lays from 6 to 16 rather large eggs. Specimens from the predominantly warm lowlands may lay multiple clutches; specimens from the cool highlands may lay but a single clutch. An eight-month-long incubation is needed at temperatures between 71° and 74°F (22°–23°C).

Note: Occasionally small, green "*brevicornis*" are offered for sale.

These are often designated as *C. b. hilleniusi.* It has been determined rather recently that instead of a subspecies of the elephant-eared chameleon, these green animals are a full species. In accordance, "*brevicornis*" should be dropped from their name and they should be called *C. hilleniusi.* The common name of "green elephant-ear" is perfectly acceptable. *C. hilleniusi* is dramatically smaller (to 7 inches; 18 cm) than *brevicornis* and is a high-altitude species. Although little is known about its breeding biology, a dead female that I dissected contained six shelled eggs.

The reproductive cycling necessary for the high-altitude members of this quartet are probably harsher than those necessary for the low-altitude specimens. There is a current trend toward supplying collecting data with imported chameleon specimens. This may well help us to set up reproductively compatible groups, as well as to know what degree and length of cooling time is necessary.

Although specimens of all have been found on the ground, the four species mentioned in this chapter are basically arboreal. Because trees and shrubs are often stressed and smaller at high altitudes, chameleons found in that habitat may be less reluctant than those from lower, forested locations to assume terrestrial positions. However, the terraria of all should contain climbing branches and live plants.

More Madagascans: Parson's, the Globe-horned, and the Tusked Chameleons

These are the three most commonly seen (and imported) of the large chameleons of Madagascar. Unfortunately, all three are also considered difficult-to-keep species and only one, the Parson's chameleon, has been bred in captivity. Even it has been bred fewer than a handful of times, and the hatching ratio of the eggs has been abysmal. Still, it *is* a start—providing we learn from our mistakes and improve on our attempts.

Despite the fact that the globe-horned and tusked chameleons are often mistaken for one another, they are not particularly closely related. The former, *Calumma globifer*, (named for the paired, globular rostral protuberances) is a member of the *C. parsonii* complex. The latter, *Furcifer balteatus*, has as its closest relatives such species as the elephant-eared and LaBord's chameleons. Its common name is derived from the attenuated, anteriorly directed, diagonal, light tusk-like marking on each side.

The nominate form of the huge Parson's chameleon probably needs no introduction. Its high-casqued head, yellow to orange eye turrets, and blunt, heavy, divergent rostral processes are a familiar sight to most hobbyists. The all-green, high-casqued, weakly crested, green eye-turreted *C. p. cristifer* is less well-known.

Parson's Chameleon

Appearance

C. p. parsonii epitomizes everything that everyone wants in a chameleon. Males are immense, attaining an overall length of more than 24 inches (61 cm). The females are somewhat smaller, attaining only about 18 inches (46 cm) in total length.

These are big, slow-moving (actually sedentary) chameleons which, when in good condition, are truly impressive. Their heavy body and precise motions impart a ponderous appearance to the creatures. Males have short, paired nasal appendages that are clad in tuberculate, enlarged scales. Females lack the nasal adornment. The body scales of both sexes are small and quite smooth.

Although it is often said that Parson's chameleon is of rather standardized color, there is actually quite a little diversity. Besides the light green to turquoise phase, red, yellow, and yellow and green morphs have been reported. The females of all morphs are often a rather brilliant green. Nonreceptive females become spotted with yellow when approached by a

A female Parson's chameleon, Calumma p. parsonii, *ambles along an arboreal pathway.*

Male Parson's chameleons, Calumma p. parsonii, *are truly impressive creatures.*

Calumma parsonii cristifer *has a slight dorsal crest.*

male. Juveniles are typically a terra-cotta color.

Typically, adult males are turquoise to light bluish-green on the sides, darker (olive-brown) vertebrally, olive-brown on both the crown of the head and the rostral processes, and often have light (gray, white, or yellow) lips.

Captive Care

Despite the fact that Parson's are not active chameleons, they do not do well in cramped quarters. They demand (and deserve) heavily planted, room-sized cages. While kept in the step-in cages (4 × 2.5 × 6 inches; 10 × 6.4 × 15 cm) that I use for other chameleon species, the *parsonii* continually displayed their discontent by almost continually attempting to escape. When moved into cages with twice the floor space, dense plant cover, and with more and larger perches, the chameleons became quiescent and began to thrive.

Despite its large size, Parson's chameleon is considered a problematic species by most herpetoculturists. However, if kept single except at breeding time, given ample space, varied prey, sufficiently high 80 to 100 percent relative humidity and suitably cool—62° to 82°F (17°–28°C) temperatures, Parson's chameleons will live apparently quite contentedly. On the other hand, if crowded or overly warm, they will quickly languish.

Semidormancy: Now that we have finally found the correct combination of factors to keep Parson's chameleons alive, we need to begin exploring the subtleties necessary to induce them to thrive and successfully breed. In the wild, Parson's chameleon is largely a cloud-forest-canopy species. In habitat, at least in parts of their range, Parson's chameleons are subjected to several weeks of cooler winter weather. These populations find a suitable perch, huddle down, and enter a period of semidormancy. They may remain quiescent on their chosen perch for days on end, moving to feed if temperatures temporarily warm and returning to their first or another suitable perch when it again becomes cool. (It is during these times that their incubating eggs experience diapause.) Perhaps this semidormancy, still lacking in most breeding programs, is more critical to the overall well-being of these magnificent lizards than we have yet acknowledged.

A globe-horned chameleon, Calumma globifer, *in passive colors. Note the coiled tail.*

Diet

Although baby specimens readily accept small feed items, the larger specimens prefer, and at times insist on, larger prey. Large beetles, moths, nonnoxious butterflies, roaches, mice, and small birds are eagerly accepted by both specimens in the wild and acclimated captives.

Eggs

Parson's chameleons have large clutches (30 to 65) of fairly large ($\frac{5}{8} \times 1$ inch; 1.5×2.5 cm) eggs. Apparently only a single clutch is produced each year. Few viable eggs have been produced by captive specimens, even by female *parsonii* gravid when wild-collected. The failure of eggs to develop is probably ours rather than that of the lizards. It would appear that even under ideal conditions, the soil temperatures at the cool, high altitudes where *parsonii* is found insure a very long incubation period. It has been suggested that at its shortest, under the very best of conditions, incubation takes a minimum of 15 months. It may actually last long beyond that, with durations of 22 months having been recorded. Successful incubation has occurred under a variety of conditions. Cool temperatures with no diapause as well as one and even two definite diapauses have been used. Ken Kalisch, who first used the two-diapause

A male tusked chameleon, Furcifer balteatus, *peers at the camera. Although it resembles* Calumma p. parsonii *and* C. globifer, *the tusked chameleon is not closely related to the two large calumma species.*

Tusked chameleons are a large and attractive Malagasy species. This is a male specimen.

method, now suspects that by so doing he merely added several additional months to what would have already been a lengthy incubation period. It is suspected that in the wild, the eggs of *C. parsonii*, undergo just the single cold-weather diapause experienced by many other high-altitude chameleons.

Note: If there is a paucity of information regarding *C. p. parsonii*, there is an absolute void regarding the smaller, more brilliantly colored *C. p. cristifer*. Adult males of this subspecies seem to top out at less than 20 inches (50 cm). Females are several inches shorter.

This form is apparently restricted to the forested areas of Perinet. The eyelids of *cristifer* are green and an anterior dorsal crest, lacking in the nominate form, is present.

The Globe-horned Chameleon

Appearance

Males of the globe-horned chameleon, *C. globifer*, another very large, basically green, eastern Madagascar species, are easily differentiated from Parson's chameleon by the short, globular rostral protuberances (those of Parson's are much longer).

Males of *C. globifer* attain a length of nearly 17 inches (43 cm). Females are several inches shorter.

Eggs

François Le Berre (1995) reports that the single annual clutch of this species contains between 30 and 50 eggs which, at 70°F or 21°C (the preferred incubation temperature), will hatch in about eight months.

This species gives the impression of being a rough-scaled species. It is only occasionally imported and virtually nothing is known of its breeding biology. Like the closely related

C. parsonii, C. globifer is a species of the cool, forested areas.

The Tusked Chameleon

Despite its similarity in appearance and large size, the tusked chameleon, *F. balteatus*, is not closely allied to the previous two large species.

Range

This species seems restricted in distribution to the central eastern part of the island.

Appearance

Males of the tusked chameleon attain a total length of nearly 19 inches (48 cm).

This species can vary from nearly unmarked bright green to a yellow-green marked prominently with darker bands. The paired rostral appendages of the males are rather long, parallel, and quite pointed. Although the light, upwardly turned, forward-directed tusklike marking may be obscure at times, it is usually very much in evidence and is indicative of the species.

Captive Care

F. balteatus is a species of the moderate elevations. The regimen of care under which it best survives is similar to that used for the Parson's and *globifer* chameleons. Cool temperatures, are required; temperatures above 78°F (26°C) should be shunned.

Eggs

A gravid, wild-collected female *F. balteatus* that I acquired deposited 34 eggs. Despite my best efforts, none developed.

Note: Much more captive care and breeding information is needed on all of the above species. Should you acquire any, I urge you to keep detailed notes and to share all information learned.

Two Small *Calumma:* The Leaf-nosed and Side-striped Chameleons

The Leaf-nosed Chameleon

The little leaf-nosed chameleon, *Calumma nasuta*, is one of the smallest of the typical arboreal chameleons. It attains a total length of just slightly more than 4 inches (10 cm).

Range

C. nasuta occurs in both primary forest and savanna habitats of eastern Madagascar. It seldom ascends more than a few feet above the ground.

Appearance

The rostral appendage from which this species takes both common and scientific name is proportionately larger and more squared on males than on females.

Both sexes are usually some shade of brown, tan, or light green. The red is often the brightest on the crown of the head and the limbs. Nonreceptive females develop bluish flash spots.

Captive Care

This interesting and very tiny typical chameleon is just beginning to be imported in fair numbers from Madagascar. Initial observations have indicated it is a hardy species if adequate quantities of sufficiently small insects are available. Captives will accept baby crickets but, like the leaf chameleons, prefer the variety offered in field plankton.

While clinging to a slender twig or vine, this chameleon species often positions itself obliquely head downward while sleeping or resting.

Eggs

Each clutch numbers from two to six eggs and healthy females may produce several clutches a year. The incubation time required is rather short, hovering right at 90 days at a temperature of 71° to 74°F (22°–23°C).

As this species becomes increasingly available, more hobbyists are developing an interest in it. Its small size allows a pair or even a trio to be kept in a 20-gallon-long tank. Once quite expensive, with greater availability the prices are now dropping quickly.

The Side-striped Chameleon

Most of what has been said above regarding pricing and care apply equally to the small side-striped chameleon, *Calumma gastrotaenia* ssp.

Range

In its eastern and central Madagascar home, *gastrotaenia* occurs at moderate elevations. *C. gastrotaenia* is

The little leaf-nosed chameleon, Calumma nasuta, *is one of the smallest of the "typical chameleons."*

The Madagascar side-striped chameleon, Calumma gastrotaenia, *is small and graceful.*

known to dwell in shrubs and low in trees in both forested areas and clearing edges. Since it blends nearly to imperceptibility in a well-planted terrarium, it should be virtually invisible in its natural habitat.

Appearance

Although males occasionally attain a length of somewhat more than 5 inches (12 cm), most are actually smaller and, because they have a long, tapering tail and slender body, all look smaller. Females are the smaller sex, seldom exceeding 4 inches (10 cm) in total length.

Captive Care

The single specimen of this type that I have kept fared rather well for several months. It ate very small feed insects and was avidly interested in termites. It drank readily and for long periods whenever the terrarium plantings were misted.

Eggs

The single clutch of which I am aware numbered three eggs and was produced by an imported female. The eggs were incubated at 72°F (23°C), but none hatched.

Subspecies

There are presently three recognized races of the side-striped chameleon, but they are not easily differentiated by external morphology. The internal differences indicate some may actually be different species rather than subspecies of *C. gastrotaenia.* For both of these reasons I will make no effort to differentiate the creatures here.

Two Large Madagascan *Furcifers*: Oustalet's and the Spiny Chameleon

Two large species of the genus *Furcifer* are the most generally distributed chameleons on Madagascar. Oustalet's chameleon, *F. oustaleti*, the world's largest species, is found virtually all over the island. The very similar appearing and only slightly smaller *F. verrucosus*, often called the spiny chameleon, is more restricted in distribution, occurring mainly in the south and western parts of the island. The two are very similar in gross external appearance and sight records placing verrucosus in the forests of the north and east may be cases of mistaken identity. Neither species has rostral adornments.

Both the spiny and Oustalet's chameleons seem to be adapting well to man's tampering with the environment. In fact, as the forests of Madagascar are methodically turned into charcoal, the range of Oustalet's chameleon is expanding. They may be seen in roadside shrubs and dooryard bushes as well as in more isolated areas.

Oustalet's Chameleon

During his trips to Madagascar, Bill Love found that Oustalet's chameleons had apparently not heard the tale that chameleons are solitary creatures. In most cases, when an Oustalet's

Although attractive, gravid female Oustalet's chameleons, Furcifer oustaleti, *are not brightly colored.*

A male spiny chameleon, Furcifer verrucosus, *shows the enlarged cheek scales that help differentiate this species from Oustalet's chameleon.*

73

chameleon was found, a second specimen (of the opposite sex) was found very close by. Love was impressed by the variety of habitats in which he found Oustalet's chameleons. He found them common in the hot, arid lowlands as well as in the cooler areas of the central plateau.

Appearance

What is an Oustalet's chameleon? Well, they're long and lanky and the males are usually some shade of brown, tan, or gray, with broad, vertical russet or deep brown bands of varying intensity. Gravid females can actually be somewhat pretty, often assuming a golden hue with dull-red bands and spots. Occasionally females may have a blush of olive-green suffusing their sides. Both a gular and a dorsal crest of small spines are present, as is a rather accentuated casque. Females are considerably smaller and have a much reduced casque. The cheek scales of this species are small.

Average-sized males are 2 feet (6.5 m) in length; large males are 27 to 28 inches (56–71 cm); exceptional males have been measured at more than 30 inches (76 cm); the largest known male measured a shade more than 32 inches (81 cm).

Captive Care

Having a particular interest in the chameleons of Madagascar, Love is making a great effort to determine whether *F. oustaleti* is as hardy and adaptable in captivity as it is in the wild. To date he has bred and hatched many in his breeding facility in hot, humid southwest Florida. This, in itself, speaks volumes for the species, for many other "hardy" chameleons cannot adapt to the hot, humid conditions in this southernmost state.

While it's true that Oustalet's chameleon aren't much in the beauty department, perhaps they will make up for this visual lack in hardiness. Although I have not bred them, I have kept Oustalet's chameleons for rather long periods of time. Despite their large size, those that I have had were not particularly interested in pinky mice, preferring instead quantities of roaches, large beetles, caterpillars, giant mealworms and other suitable insect fare.

Eggs

Furcifer oustaleti from high altitudes produce only a single large clutch of eggs annually. The eggs can number more than 40. At a temperature of 74°F (23°C), incubation can last for more than nine months. The low-altitude examples of this species may, and I emphasize the may, have two clutches annually. The egg clutches of specimens from lower elevations may also average more in number, occasionally including more than 60 eggs. At 80°F (27°C), these eggs will hatch in about seven months.

The Spiny Chameleon

Range

Although both Oustalet's and the spiny chameleon may be found in more arid areas of Madagascar, the latter also occurs in forested regions. It is most common in and along clearing edges and in roadside shrubbery.

Appearance

Males tend to be dark green on the anterior portion of the trunk, with the serrate doral crest beginning behind the head. On the females, the crest tapers and ends at mid-body. Distinct large scales cover the body surfaces of both sexes. Light colored, blotchy side marking occur on some males. The large casque is slightly more oblong than oustaleti's. The females' overall coloration is darker than the males.

Like Oustalet's chameleon, the spiny chameleon is big and rather slender. Adult males may exceed 22 inches (55 cm) in total length. Females are about eight inches (21 cm).

Captive Care

These large chameleons are relatively active and should be provided with large cages. Both bask extensively and should be provided with warmed, illuminated, hot spots. If possible, move their cages outside on warm sunny days. If the cages are of wood and wire construction, the cages can be left out day and night during the warmer months of the year. In southwest Florida, I kept both species outdoors year around. During the cold winter nights their cages were wrapped in heavy plastic film and warmth was provided by ceramic heating units.

While not of brilliant colors, I have found both the Oustalet's and spiny chameleons alert and responsive. While two males cannot be housed together, if their cages are large enough, sexual pairs (or trios) seem to do quite well.

Eggs

Egg clutch size is fairly small—from 10 to 15 eggs. At 72°F (22°C), the incubation time for the eggs of *F. verrucosus*, is about seven months.

Both Oustalet's and the spiny chameleon bask extensively. In climatically inhospitable areas, both may brumate for several weeks. Unlike Parson's chameleon which merely finds a suitable branch and hunkers down, both the Oustalet's and spiny chameleons reportedly dig shallow burrows in which to brumate. Their caging should provide for this option.

Of the two, I have personally found Oustalet's chameleon to be somewhat the hardier.

Given the current trend of supplying collecting data with the chameleons that are imported, it should be rather easy for a hobbyist to find the specimens, even in a single genus such as *Furcifer*, best suited for his or her particular climate. For instance, should you dwell in southern Florida or the lower Rio Grande valley, you should request lowland specimens that are better adapted to heat than those from the highlands. If you live in more northerly areas, perhaps highland specimens, more adapted to coolness, would better suit your needs.

Four *Chamaeleos*: The Common, Flap-necked, Graceful, and Senegal Chameleons

I have always found it strange that reptiles and amphibians that are kept with ease by herpetoculturists in one country are those considered difficult by hobbyists in another country.

This is the case with the four chameleon species listed above. European hobbyists have told me time and again "no problem," and their breeding records would seem to attest to this. However, in the United States none of these four are considered hardy and, indeed, most are thought to be rather delicate.

Males of the graceful, Senegal, and flap-necked chameleons are extremely aggressive, not only to others of their own species, but, because they are so closely allied, to those of the other species in this chapter as well. Family groups of one male to three females (of the same species), if healthy and housed in large cages, seem compatible.

These four chameleon species, all members of the genus *Chamaeleo*, are of rather similar external appearance.

The Common Chameleon

Range

Although several races of *Chamaeleo chamaeleon* have been described, without collecting data all are virtually impossible to identify.

Often called the European or common chameleon, this is the only member of the genus to stray that far northward. In Europe it is known to occur in Portugal, Spain, and on numerous islands. It occurs also over much of North Africa and western Asia Minor. The majority of the specimens currently seen in the American pet trade are being shipped from Egypt.

Appearance

The common chameleon is variably colored and specimens from some populations show a rather marked degree of color-changing ability. However, for the most part specimens from more arid habitats have a ground color of tan or gray, while those from areas of greater rainfall may display greens and olives. Whatever the ground color, *C. chamaeleon* usually has two light (often white) longitudinal stripes on each side. These light stripes may be intact, but more often are broken into a series of dashes or spots. A well-defined light gular and ventral crest is present. The dorsal crest consists of rather small serrate scales.

The common chameleon has a well-developed casque that is highest posteriorly. The lizard lacks any additional head ornamentation. It varies in adult

There is little dimorphism in the common chameleons, Chamaeleo chamaeleon. The pair pictured here is from Egypt.

size from about 9 to slightly more than 12 inches (23–31 cm).

Breeding

This species typically has a chameleonlike attitude—asocial—but I have not found it to be quite as irascible as is often related. A single male and three females survived as a colony (along with a breeding colony of Standing's day geckos) in a large step-in cage in our facility, and two of the females produced egg clutches. Although up to 50 eggs are reportedly possible, one of our females produced two clutches of 13 and 21 eggs and the second produced a single clutch of 10 eggs. At "room temperature" in Florida (probably from 74° to 78°F, 23°–26°C) the two clutches hatched after seven and nine months of incubation, respectively. The longer time span was by a clutch that overwintered at the lower temperatures mentioned. Female common chameleons that are not sexually receptive assume a spotted coloration and a more aggressive than usual attitude if approached by the male. The spots may be yellow on green, or tan on gray-green.

Flap-necked chameleons, Chamaeleo dilepis, *have proven delicate in America.*

The graceful chameleon, Chamaeleo gracilis, *is inexpensive but delicate.*

Hibernation

The common chameleons from the more northerly (temperate) areas of the range hibernate during the winter months. Specimens from further south may become dormant both during periods of cold and excessive heat/drought. I consider this species moderately hardy, but most definitely not a beginner's chameleon.

The Flap-necked Chameleon

Range

The flap-necked chameleon, *C. dilepis*, ranges widely in forest and savanna habitats over much of tropical and southern Africa. Its common name is derived from the proportionately large, medially divided occipital lobes. The lobes are movable and a displaying adult may hold the flaps at almost right angles to the head, an impressive sight.

Appearance

Flap-necks are quite similar to the common chameleon in appearance, but have more prominently developed gular and ventral crests. The two continue uninterruptedly from chin to the midventral area. The light (often white) ventrolateral line is usually well developed on this species. It begins just posterior to the apex of the forelimb and runs diagonally upward to a point above the rear limbs. The light dorsolateral line is only weakly evident at best. Ground color may be green, tan, or brown. Males have a small tarsal protuberance and the interstitial throat skin is yellow to orange.

In this chameleon species it is the female that is the larger. A total length of 13 inches (33 cm) is commonly attained and occasional females have been measured at slightly more than 15 inches (38 cm).

Breeding

In the wild this is a prolific chameleon species. One or two clutches that number from 15 to 60 eggs are produced by large females. The incubation duration has been reported as lasting from nine to ten months at temperatures of from 78° to 83°F (26°–28°C). Sexually receptive females assume a pattern of light spots on a green ground color.

Hatchlings

The few hatchlings of this species that I have seen have varied from a nearly unicolored light green to a prominently barred green and olive-black. The hatchlings were quite pretty and did not seem overly nervous, although this is not true for the adults. I have found the flap-necked chameleons I kept nervous and easily stressed—in fact I have failed dismally at acclimating this species.

The Graceful Chameleon

Range

The third member of this group is the graceful chameleon, *C. gracilis*, a species widely spread throughout tropical Africa. It is another moderately sized species (about 12 inches or 30 cm long) and seems to be slightly less nervous than the closely allied flap-neck. Unfortunately, the graceful chameleon often succumbs soon after import to heavy loads of nematodes.

Appearance

This lizard has yellow to blue-green coloration with a pale band on each side, and grows to about 12 inches (31 cm) in length. It may assume varying hues of tan, brown, and green, and the interstitial gular skin of the males is often a brilliant yellow to orange. When displaying males inflate their throats, the brilliant interstitial skin becomes prominently visible.

The body hue becomes a much brighter green, and broad vertical bars and spots of dark olive-black or jet black appear. These displays are used in both territorial and courtship situations. The males of one subspecies of the graceful chameleon (*C. g. etiennei*) lack tarsal spurs. The tarsal spurs are prominent on males of the nominate race.

Eggs

At 77° to 80°F (25°–27°C) the 22 to 50 eggs of the graceful chameleon will hatch in somewhat more than seven months. The hatchlings seem much hardier and less nervous than the adults.

I consider this another of the difficult species. Despite its ready availability and low cost in America, I cannot recommend it. European hobbyists seem to be much more successful with graceful chameleons than their American counterparts.

The Senegal Chameleon

Range

Like the graceful chameleon, the Senegal chameleon (*C. senegelensis*) is widely distributed in tropical Africa. It reaches an overall length of 12 inches (30 cm).

Appearance

The ground color of this species varies from green to tan to olive with a profusion of dark leopard spots. There appears to be two subspecies and the males may or may not have tarsal spurs. The casque of this species is very small and low.

Eggs

A few eggs of this species have been hatched. The eggs are almost invariably laid by wild-collected females or are excised from freshly dead wild-collected females. The incubation of the 20 to 60 eggs takes about six months at 77°F (25°C). In the wild, Senegal chameleons apparently lay at least two clutches a season.

Captive-hatched babies seem much more amenable to caged conditions than the adults. This is probably because the babies lack the parasite loads and have not been stressed by collecting and shipping. The very few hatchlings that I have seen have eaten readily and grown quickly.

Note: Because they are abundant and inexpensive, the Senegal, graceful, and flap-necked chameleons have been popular in the pet trade. Unfortunately, the chance of long-term success with these three is slight (and only a bit better for the common chameleon). These are four species that I would not recommend to beginning hobbyists, and unless captive-hatched, would not even suggest them to advanced herpetoculturists. There simply are too many other chameleon species that are better suited to captive conditions.

If you are inclined to try your hand at imported specimens, do everything possible to ease any stressful conditions. Initially, keep each chameleon entirely isolated from others, offer easily digested foods, vitamins and minerals. Be extremely careful to avoid oversupplementation with vitamins and be certain that the lizards remain properly hydrated. If it finally looks as if you have a chance with them, have a veterinarian do a fecal float to determine the endoparasites present, and treat as necessary. Females that are gravid (as most imported adults are) are even more delicate and difficult to acclimatize than males. If your female is gravid and should die, remove the eggs immediately. Handle them very carefully, dry them even more carefully, and incubate as suggested in the chapter on reproduction.

Two African Chameleons: Meller's and Fischer's Chameleons

Meller's Chameleon

The first truly large chameleon that I ever saw was the very prettily colored Meller's chameleon, *Chamaeleo melleri*. In the early 1970s a fairly large shipment of these magnificent and brightly colored creatures arrived from Tanzania.

After that initial importation, Meller's chameleons disappeared again from the pet trade within the United States. Once in a while 10 or 20 of the animals would appear, but no serious numbers were available. Their prices remained high—so high, in fact, that they actually remained out of the reach of many herpetoculturists.

Over the years, a few people acquired *melleri*. Of the few that had them, some even bred them. But it was not until the very late eighties and early nineties that more Meller's chameleons became available in the general pet trade. And at that time, although still expensive, the price dropped somewhat. But even better, by the eighties we had learned a little about the keeping of chameleons, and those that became available then fared much better than earlier importations.

The largest of the specimens were a full 2 feet (6.5 m) in length; none were less than 20 inches (51 cm).

Appearance

All were clad in a ground color that varied from a green so dark that it appeared almost black, through deep forest green, to a bright leaf green. All were prominently barred and spotted with bright yellow. Whenever they sat quietly, their tails were immediately tightly coiled like so many watchsprings. The huge occipital lobes were strongly divided and the forehead sloped gently downward to a bulbous nose that had just the slightest of rostral protuberances.

Although often called the "giant one-horned chameleon," the rostral extension borne by most *C. melleri* is a pretty poor excuse for a "horn" (the horn development may be variable by populations—some specimens **do** have short, thick, annulated rostral horns.) The big lizards also had prominent, serrate, dorsal crests. Those chameleons really were something!

Captive Care

Chamaeleo melleri not only attains a length greater than that of any other African chameleon species, it is also proportionately heavy-bodied. Its diet in the wild includes all manner of suitably sized nonnoxious insects and probably the nestlings of any small bird or rodent species the lizards

Bright colors and large size make Meller's chameleons, Chamaeleo melleri, *a species coveted by enthusiasts.*

This is what you will see if you are ever nose to horn with an adult male Meller's chameleon.

happen across. Certainly, captives show a fondness for pinky mice in addition to the usual insects.

As with all of my larger chameleon species, the Meller's were housed in outside step-in cages. These are of wood and wire construction and measure 4 × 2.5 × 6 (90 × 75 × 180 cm). They are crisscrossed with branches of varying diameter and contain either one or two large potted ficus trees. The trees offer the chameleons seclusion as well as providing them with visual barriers.

Although *C. melleri* is often referred to as a cool-weather chameleon, this does not seem to be true. The species is, apparently, most common in and around savanna habitat and is not at all debilitated by temperatures in the upper eighties to very low nineties (26°–34°C). When temperatures drop into the sixties and seventies (17°–25°C) Meller's chameleons bask for long periods.

Breeding

I had always considered Meller's chameleons difficult to sex with a great degree of accuracy. Even fully grown males often had rather small and insignificant hemipenial bulges. One day, while looking with Rob MacInnes and Bill Love at a group of *C. melleri* imported by Mike Ellard, MacInnes showed me what he claimed was an accurate method of sexing the species. On the underside of their occipital flaps some of the specimens bore one or more black spots. These, MacInnes said, were the males. Upon returning home, I checked the occipital flaps of my pair of *melleri*. The specimen that I knew to be the male had the dark spots; the female lacked them. Whether this method is truly failsafe, I can't say. However, it has held true on the specimens that I have inspected.

Eggs

An imported female Mellers' chameleon that I had deposited a clutch of 3 fertile and about 30 infertile eggs. Only one of the fertile eggs developed and hatched, the gray and black baby emerging after a more than seven-month incubation. The eggs were retained at room temperature, not incubated. In southwest Florida room temperature is from 70° to 80°F (21°–27°C).

Fischer's Chameleon

We now meet a second African chameleon that in most of its several subspecies truly *does* have "nose horns" that are worthy of the name "horn." Some adult males of the African Fischer's chameleons (*Bradypodion f. fischeri*) have what may be the most accentuated rostral process known in all of chameleondom. (The rostral process is entirely lacking in at least one subspecies).

You may see references to as many as six subspecies of Fischer's chameleons. You may also see them referred to as either the genus *Chamaeleo* or the genus *Bradypodion*. Confusion reigns because Fischer's chameleons are not only greatly variable by subspecies, but they are even variable within a given subspecies (some individuals may bear nasal appendages, others may not). For our purposes, we will refer to them as members of the genus *Bradypodion*. Please note that, despite what has been written elsewhere, Fischer's chameleons are an oviparous—an egg-laying—species.

Range

These chameleons are found in tropical Africa.

Appearance

At adulthood, males of Fischer's chameleons may be small (12 to

13 inches or 30–33 cm) or large (16 to 19 inches or 45–49 cm). As often as not a dull brown, Fischer's are with or without vertical banding. At times they may assume a leaf or forest green, again with or without bands.

Captive Care

If not debilitated by collecting and transportation trauma, Fischer's chameleons can be fairly hardy captives. In the wild they range from cool, high-elevation forest habitat to lower savanna areas that are considerably warmer. If you decide to work with *B. fischeri*, watch your specimens very carefully until you determine the exact regimen of temperature and humidity necessary for your animals. If they show distress at warm temperatures, lower the temperature in increments of one or two degrees at a time. If they begin looking dry and uncomfortable, increase the relative humidity in your cage by misting. Fischer's chameleons from damp forested habitats probably bask less than others from more open savanna habitats. Experiment with basking temperatures and the usage of basking areas by your chameleons, as well. Record your findings, listing everything about your lizards that you possibly can. Some dealers (especially specialist reptile importers) may be able to provide you with some bits and pieces of collecting data. Such particulars are seldom if ever available from a pet store. If such data are available, be certain to include them.

The caging for your Fischer's chameleons will need to vary by the number and size of the specimens with which you are working. In a large cage a single male and three or four females will coexist well. In a smaller cage, a similar group may be entirely incompatible, requiring that each specimen be caged individually.

Diet

Suitably sized insects are eagerly accepted by healthy Fischer's chameleons. Although I have never offered them pinky mice, some of the larger specimens of Fischer's chameleons should certainly be able to eat and digest these. Remember to dust the feed insects with vitamin D_3 and calcium additives.

Breeding

Do not think you can use the presence of horns to determine the sexes of these chameleons. Both sexes of *B. f. excubitor* lack horns. While the males of the other subspecies usually have horns, they may be large or small. This may be reversed with females, most lacking horns but some females of some subspecies having them. The hemipenial bulges of the males are a more reliable method of sexing Fischer's chameleons.

As I have tried to demonstrate, variability is the keynote even within a given subspecies of Fischer's chameleon. Without precise collecting data (not often available with African chameleons), to try to assign a Fischer's chameleon to a subspecies is an exercise in futility.

Eggs

Fischer's chameleons lay one or more clutches of from 10 to 35 (usually 18 to 24) eggs. Like the care given the chameleons themselves, the care necessary to induce proper development of the eggs will vary. Eggs from high-elevation adults will need to be incubated at cooler temperatures than eggs from lower elevation specimens. If, even after succeeding this far with your adults, you remain unsure of the proper temperatures, err on the side of coolness. Consider 68° to 70°F (19°–21°C) the temperature range at which you will most likely be successful. The eggs of

The appearance of Fischer's chameleon, Bradypodion fischeri, *varies by subspecies.*

Bradypodion fischeri multituberculatus *is one of the largest African rainforest chameleons.*

low-elevation *B. fischeri* have been successfully incubated at 75°F (24°C). At that temperature, development took slightly longer than five months. Incubation would probably have been as successful, but would have taken longer at 70°F.

Note: Because of the complexities involving the systematics of Fischer's chameleons, I would strongly suggest obtaining all of your specimens at the same time. Often most of the specimens imported together will have been collected from the same general location. It is more likely that your specimens will be genetically compatible if this is the case.

Fischer's chameleons are subtly attractive and reasonably hardy. They are a species with which dedicated hobbyists should be able to succeed.

Studies in Green: The Cameroon Mountain and the Four-horned Chameleon

Female Chamaeleo montium *are not always as dark as this specimen.*

The light colored dorsal bars of female four-horned chameleons, Chamaeleo quadricornis, *are usually easily visible.*

The male Cameroon mountain chameleon, C. montium, is a beautiful creature. The species thrives in the cool, humid, high-altitude forests of Cameroon in West Africa.

Adult males of the four-horned chameleon, C. quadricornis, often have two tiny horns posterior to the four larger ones.

Green. It's one of my favorite colors. But there are some shades that I like better than others—and the greens in which these two tropical West African chameleon species are clad are the bright shades of new leaves. But it's not color alone that catches my eye, for the chameleons themselves are spectacular.

Of course, the fixing superlatives to characteristics perceived differently by different viewers is difficult and smacks of anthropomorphism. But if that's the case, I'm guilty when it comes to two chameleons: the Cameroon mountain, *Chamaeleo* (*Trioceros*) *montium*, and the four-horned, *C.* (*T.*) *quadricornis*. The additional term in parentheses, *Trioceros*, is a subgenus. The "parent" genus *Chamaeleo* has been split into two subgenera, *Trioceros* and *Chamaeleo*.

Until recently *C. quadricornis* was considered a rare chameleon. Since the late 1980s, though, several small shipments of both this species and *montium* have arrived in the United States and Europe. Although *C. quadricornis* is said by some authors to be a species of savanna-edge habitat, other authorities claim it to be a species of cool, wet forest habitat.

Range

Some taxonomists feel that besides the nominate forms of each, *C. montium* is represented by three additional forms and *quadricornis* by one. For our purposes we will ignore that possibility. Both *C. montium* and *C. quadricornis* are montane chameleons from the country of Cameroon (Cameroun) in West Africa.

Appearance

The mountain chameleon is a species of humid, cool, high-altitude forests. It is somewhat darker than the four-horned chameleon and the arrangement of the horns is very different. Male montium have only two large horns. Initially, these diverge slightly, then curve and are directed straight forward for their distal half.

On the other hand, the horns of the quite inappropriately named four-horned chameleon are proportionately shorter. This species actually has three pairs of horns on the snout. Of graduated size, the longest pair are anteriormost in the sequence and are directed upward. The posterior pair may be nothing more than an enlargement of single nasal scales on each side of the snout. The middle pair are of intermediate length and often directed slightly outward.

The males of both species have rather low, prominently ribbed vertebral crests which continue to and proportionately heighten on the basal third of the tail. It is from these crests that both species derive a secondary pet-store name—sailfin chameleon.

When content, the males of both the mountain and the four-horned chameleons are clad in scales of lime green (at times bordering on chartreuse) with highlights of yellow, turquoise, robin's-egg blue, and terracotta or peach. These highlights are often most pronounced dorsally and anteriolaterally. Entire or broken, broad, white, dorsolateral bands may or may not be evident. It would seem that these bands are invariably evident on sleeping specimens. Specimens that are too warm, too cold, or otherwise stressed are usually quite dark, lack the colorful highlights, and may even show evidence of darker banding.

The females of both have only vestiges, if anything, to represent the horns and may have broad white crossbands dorsally. Females that have been introduced to males but are not receptive to breeding often darken to nearly black in overall coloration.

The males of both species are nearly a foot in total length; the females are two to three inches shorter.

Captive Care

Both the mountain and the four-horned chameleon do reasonably well as captives if provided with the proper regimen of care and terrarium parameters. Although coming from a country which lies only a few degrees north of the equator, the elevations at which the mountain and four-horned chameleons occur assure that both species are perpetually cool. At the upper end of the seventies (25°C), both begin to show signs of discomfort; if allowed to go above the very low eighties (27°C), both species become acutely distressed. The rainfall in their mountain homes is also considerable, though to a degree seasonal. There are two pronounced rainy seasons, broken by two poorly defined "dry" seasons. The term "dry" is a comparison only and if taken literally would be a misnomer. The temperatures of these mountain fastnesses range from the high fifties to the very low eighties (14°–28°C). As might be surmised, the nearly daily rains assure a very high relative humidity in these mountain forests, and the nearly continual cloud covers prevent all but intermittent sunlight. These are conditions which should be duplicated in the terrarium. Even when provided with a basking lamp, the specimens which I have kept have shown little inclination to use it.

When sleeping, both of these chameleons lower their heads to the branch on which they are sitting and coil the tail into a tight watchspring. At this time they are in appearance very much like a broad, pale-green leaf.

I have not been able to find any literature relating to the territorial needs of these species in the wild. In captivity, neither species is particularly active. I have maintained both for extensive periods in 20-gallon "high" terraria. Although many authors have suggested keeping the sexes separate, I have seen no adverse interactions when they are maintained as pairs or trios. Of the two, *C. montium* seems the more aggressive. Hatchlings can also be kept communally. Until sexual maturity is attained, baby males seem no more aggressive than females. If you do maintain these creatures communally, you must take the time to ascertain that all are getting their share of the food insects. As with many reptiles, there will be some specimens that feed more readily than others.

Diet

It is important when feeding these two chameleon species that suitably sized insects are used. Individual large insects, as well as large meals of smaller insects can induce regurgitation. Small meals of comparatively small insects fed at frequent intervals seem the best for these interesting and very beautiful chameleons.

Eggs

Both mountain and four-horned chameleons are oviparous. Females have rather small clutches (typically from 5 to 12, rarely to 16) of fairly large eggs. At a temperature of from 70° to 72°F (21°–22°C), incubation durations vary from four and a half to just under six months. It is not uncommon for all hatchlings to emerge within a few hours of each other. The hatchlings are about an inch and a half in length and will begin eating termites and pinhead crickets within a few hours of hatching. If amply fed, the growth of the young of both species is rapid. They have been known to reach sexual maturity within a a period of seven months.

The Dwarf Chameleons: The *Bradypodion pumilum* Group

The dwarf chameleons are another group of chameleons in a state of taxonomic flux. Which species are considered members of the genus *Bradypodion*, or whether the genus is even entirely valid, will be entirely dependent on which researcher is being quoted. For the purpose of this publication we will be discussing some of the live-bearing South African members of what is often termed the "*pumilum*" group. (*Pumilum* refers to a group of chameleons that appear to be very closely allied to

B. *pumilum*.) The *pumilum* group (or complex) consists of about 13 species, but this number is subject to change as research continues.

Although dwarf chameleons were once imported from South Africa in fair numbers for the American pet trade, the various species are now seldom seen on dealer lists. There are, however, a number of private breeders who are successfully working with one or more species and a few babies are available to dedicated hobbyists each year.

Range

Most of the many members of this genus are found in very restricted areas in South Africa, at or near the coast. Several species are considered vulnerable, threatened or endangered by the South African conservation authorities, however none are yet listed on the Endangered Species List. All are protected by the South African Government and like the rest of the chameleons (except *Brookesia* and *Rhampholeon*), are listed by CITES. Because of their extremely limited ranges, habitat degradation is a constant threat for many *Bradypodion*.

Appearance

The members of the *pumilum* complex of the genus *Bradypodion* are all

The Natal-Midlands dwarf chameleon,
Bradypodion thamnobates, *in profile.*

of rather standardized appearance. All are relatively small, being from 11 to 15 inches (28–38 cm). All have gular crests, all have casques (the casques of some species are very prominent), all have dorsal crests of serrate scales, and all have series of prominently enlarged, tuberculate scales on the flanks and limbs.

It is the male of the species in this genus that develops the most intense hues and complex patterns during the breeding season. They assume ground colors of green which are either suffused or boldly patterned laterally with strawberry, pink, gold, or tan. The females of many species remain gray, tan, or reddish but may assume lighter colors suffused with pinks or light greens.

The Natal-Midlands dwarf chameleon is capable of assuming many colors, but the pattern of those colors is standardized.

Captive Care

These are wonderfully hardy chameleons that are well adapted to relatively hostile climatic and environmental conditions. Most members of the genus *Bradypodion* are very territorial. Males are especially so, and more than one should not be kept to an enclosure. Females are somewhat less antagonistic, and several may be kept together if the cage is large and well planted (or has numerous other visual barriers). Hierarchies will be established, and the lizard lowest in the pecking order may rapidly become debilitated. If this lowest-ranking specimen is removed, the next lowest will then receive the accumulated aggression. It is even necessary to monitor carefully the interactions of the male dwarf chameleon with the females. Aggression can sometimes occur.

As might be expected, aggressive interactions are apt to be more severe in small cages than in large.

The most successful captive breeding programs for dwarf chameleons in America are those formulated by Bert and Hester Langerwerf. In their

large facility in central Alabama, groups of the Natal midlands dwarf chameleons live, thrive, and interact much the same as they would in nature. The cages are open to the elements in all but the most severe of winter weather. In these large cages, the chameleons readily produce with what may be termed normal fecundity, the Langerwerfs finding more than 100 baby chameleons a season.

The Natal Midlands Dwarf Chameleon

Although it was once one of the most infrequently seen, *B. thamnobates*, the Natal midlands dwarf chameleon, is the species that is now the most often offered to hobbyists.

Range

B. thamnobates is of very restricted distribution in South Africa, being found in the Natal midlands in extreme eastern South Africa.

Appearance

The males of this species have a high tan, or tan and blue casque, and usually a light throat. The dorsal crest is studded with enlarged scales, and the gular crest is prominent. Ventrolateral, posterior, and caudal and limb scalation is very coarse and rugose. When not in breeding colors, the male is mostly deep forest green. This may have a bluish tinge ventrolaterally and posteriorly. The anterior sides usually have a poorly delineated bar of white, tan, yellow, pink, or strawberry discernible. All colors are very much brighter when the male is in breeding colors.

Females are lighter, often tan, gray, or light green.

Thamnobates is one of the larger members of the group. Adult males attain a total length of somewhat more than 7 inches (18 cm). The females are considerably smaller.

Captive Care

These little chameleons are hardy if not subjected to undue heat. They become distressed when summer temperatures rise above 85°F (29.4°C), especially when this is coupled with very high humidity. Chameleons of this species can tolerate freezing temperatures for short periods of time. In normally colder areas, this, and other species, brumate for several weeks each winter.

Neonates

As with all *Bradypodion*, clutches can be large and the newly born babies very tiny. Despite having a rather lengthy gestation period (3 to 4 months), several clutches of young can be produced annually by adult females. Tremendous amounts of very small food insects are required to raise the babies. Vitamin D_3 and calcium additives are mandatory during periods of rapid growth and should be continued, at least sporadically, for the life of the lizard. Because of winter cold, it often takes the various *Bradypodion* well over a year to become sexually mature.

The Cape Dwarf Chameleon

The Cape dwarf chameleon, *B. pumilum*, once so common in the pet trade, is now very seldom seen outside of its native South Africa. A few European breeders continue to work with this species.

Appearance

Although as large as the Natal midlands dwarf chameleon, the Cape dwarf chameleon has much smoother scalation and a lighter ground color than *B. thamnobates*. The anteriolateral marking, often bright and well delineated, may vary from a very pretty yellow-ochre to strawberry.

The Leaf Chameleons:
The Tolerant *Brookesia*

Above my desk is a shelf. On that shelf is a 20-gallon-long terrarium set up with a crisscrossed maze of slender branches and a thick substrate of dead crumbled leaves. From where I sit, all this looks like an absolutely impenetrable maze. Anybody looking in the tank would wonder why I would bother to have a tank of leaves sitting there. The fact that I have just misted the tank raises another question. Why bother to water a tank of dead leaves? The leaves are those of wax myrtle and live oak, all clad in warm hues of brown. The wax myrtle leaves are elongate with weakly serrate edges. The oak leaves are smooth-edged ellipsoids.

Above the tank are two lights. One, a 50-watt incandescent plant grow-bulb, shines downward illuminating and gently warming a small patch of leaves below it. The other light, a fluorescent fixture, holds a small Vita-lite tube. Although when compared to sunlight its output is weak, the Vita-lite is a full-spectrum bulb which emits minuscule amounts of UV-A and UV-B, both considered beneficial rays. So now we have a 20-gallon tank busily appointed in slender twigs, with a carpet of leaves, overhead illumination, and which has just been misted. In the brilliance of the bulbs the water droplets dangle, prismatically pendulant, shimmering in rainbow colors. Slowly, ever so slowly, one of the bigger leaves opens a black eye, stretches upward, and begins—to drink. The shimmering droplet disappears. The leaf moves slowly to the next droplet and the scenario is repeated.

A baby cricket moves. Dusted in vitamin/calcium powder, it appears ghostly white against the brown leaves. It nears the large drinking leaf and begins to ascend a thin twig. Upward—upward—it's almost at the top, when zap! In a flash of pink the cricket disappears. The leaf's black eye rotates around, scanning to the back, the front, the side, upward, downward. I sit, nose glued to the terrarium glass, word processor temporarily forgotten.

The leaf begins to move again, ahead a step, a shudder as if breeze-blown, another step ahead. The leaf turns. Now I can see both eyes and a short, blunt tail that resembles nothing so much as a stem. The leaf turns more. Now visible are ribs that look like leaf veins and a series of dorso-lateral projections that serve to disrupt its outline even more. The leaf moves forward slowly, haltingly, stopping for another drink, stopping again to catch a couple of termites, then another small cricket catches its eye. The leaf seems almost to rush forward. Then, zap. Another cricket gone.

Two shoebutton eyes, a short tail, brown sides, tan back, jagged dorso-lateral projections—what I had before me was a Thiel's leaf chameleon, *Brookesia thieli*, a mite of a lizard that, with another species of the genus, the horned-leaf chameleon, *B. supercil-iaris*, had just arrived from

Brookesia thieli *almost disappears against a substrate of leaves.*

Although not accomplished climbers, Brookesia superciliaris *does ascend low bushes.*

Brookesia minima *is the world's smallest chameleon species.*

Madagascar. Now a pair of each dwelt in the tank above my desk. These two *Brookesia* were my introduction to these minuscule Madagascan masters of mimicry. Had I not *known* them to be there I wouldn't have even suspected their presence. Even knowing them to be there, I was seldom able to find them without spending quite some time looking. And this was in an area 12 × 30 inches (31 × 76 cm)—just 360 square inches. I could only imagine the difficulty I would have had finding the creatures in nature.

That the *Brookesia* had come to be in this tank was more or less accidental. Rob MacInnes had called a few days earlier and told me that he was receiving some unusual chameleons. He was wondering whether I might like to photograph some? So about midnight that night, I packed the photographic gear into the car and scooted on over to Rob's. Rob and crew were unpacking a large and most interesting Madagascan shipment, and as they unpacked I took photo after photo. Reptile species, both large and small, that I knew only from literature were in that shipment, and toward the end of the unpacking, a few of those species turned out to be the *Brookesia*—the leaf chameleons.

At very first sight I was enchanted by these benign appearing little beings and, being an inquisitive sort, there was never any question that when I left, some of the *Brookesia* would leave with me.

And now, days later, I sat watching their every action, wondering whether I was doing things correctly for the lizards and knowing full well that it was still much too early to tell.

But at least I was learning that in their slow, cryptic manner the chameleons were active. I had seen them drinking, I had seen them eating. Early every morning, when the lights were first turned on, the chameleons would awaken, ever so slowly, and even more slowly clamber upward, hand over hand, in a manner curiously unsteady for a "sure-footed" chameleon, to elevated positions where they could warm themselves. Once that was accomplished, they would return to the lowest limbs or the substrate itself and begin hunting. Equally as curious as anything else that the chameleons did was their entire lack of animosity toward one another. As you have probably noted in previous pages, chameleons in general are not noted for their placidity toward others of their own, or even closely allied, species. Yet these little *Brookesia* basked closely to one another and often shot crickets while only inches apart. They took little note of visual barriers and would prowl in apparent contentment within complete sight of each other. I really decided that the specimens I had were not at all antagonistic when one morning three of the four positioned themselves at various places on a single branch and all fed voraciously on the vitamin-dusted crickets that wandered within tongue-shot.

I mist the chameleon enclosure twice daily, in the morning when the lights are first turned on and in the late afternoon. The chameleons seem to drink most copiously in the morning. They also seem to feed most readily in the morning.

The leaf chameleon that is most unique in appearance is Brookesia perarmata, *a species which may feed largely on ants.*

Rhampholeon kersteni *is the most frequently seen of the African leaf chameleons.*

Range

With the single exception of the armored leaf chameleon, all members of both the genera *Brookesia* of Madagascar and *Rhampholeon* of mainland Africa favor areas of humid, primary forests and according to species, may be either lowland or montane forest dwellers. In contrast, the armored leaf chameleon favors the dry, rocky ("tsingy," pronounced just

as it's spelled) eroded limestone areas of western central Madagascar. In this habitat of warm temperatures and low humidity, leaf chameleons occur in vegetation amid and surrounding the rocky pinnacles.

Although currently being subjectively scrutinized, at present the Madagascan genus *Brookesia* numbers 22 species. The African genus *Rhampholeon* includes about 10 species.

Appearance

Although the very word "chameleon" connotes dramatic color changes, neither the little *Brookesia* nor the closely allied *Rhampholeon* are capable of much color change. Most are clad in scales of brown and/or tan. Some, especially those that frequent mossy tree trunks and limbs, also have patches of moss green. Since for the most part these are creatures of the shadows, whether forest floor or mossy trunk, the browns, tans, and moss greens afford these chameleons nearly perfect camouflage. The ventral coloration of some species may be brighter than the dorsal colors.

Captive Care

Although I have not crowded them, I have successfully kept them in tanks (enclosures) proportionately smaller than those that I would use for the more active arboreal chameleons. Although I initially kept four or five specimens in each 20-gallon-long tank, I soon decided to double the size of the individual terraria. I did this by removing an endglass from two 20-gallon tanks and abutting them. The juncture can be sealed with tape or silicone aquarium sealant. The stand on which the tanks are placed must be sturdy and long enough to be able to hold the two tanks end to end. The same space can be given by removing a side glass from two aquaria and placing them front to back. However I found that I liked the elongated area better than the wider one. Although I have always kept a very shallow dish of water in the terrarium, I have never seen these lizards drink anything except the droplets of mist from the branches and leaves.

Diet

As I would for any reptile or amphibian, I suggest as varied a diet as is possible for these little chameleons. Over the years mine have readily accepted not only the tiny crickets and termites mentioned earlier, but baby mealworms, small sowbugs, fruit-flies and mixed, suitably sized field plankton as well. At times aphid infestations provide an additional source of food. Since these latter insects often tend to accumulate in vast numbers on the soft-growing tips of stems, it is an easy chore to merely snip the twig free and place the entire thing in the leaf chameleon terrarium.

Eggs

All members of both genera are oviparous. The embryos of many are in a rather advanced developmental stage prior to the eggs being laid. Several clutches a year, that number from one to five eggs per clutch, are laid by the adult females. Incubation is rather short, hatching occurring in many cases in four to nine weeks subsequent to the deposition date. Depending on normal habitat conditions, the incubation temperatures suggested for captives varies from 68° to 74°F (20°–23°C). The eggs of the lowland forms should be incubated at the warmer temperatures.

The tails of all members of this subfamily are moderately prehensile at best and nonprehensile at worst.

Let's take a look at a few of these interesting but little-known and little-studied species. Since none have anything but contrived common names, if available I will use the names that I have seen most frequently on the various price lists.

Thiel's Leaf Chameleon

Brookesia thieli is a moderately sized species, attaining a total length of about 2¾ inches (7 cm). A small but well-defined nasal protuberance is present. The dorsolateral projections number 11 on each side. The supraorbital projections are directed anteriorly and quite sharp.

The Horned Leaf Chameleon

The supraorbital projections of the horned leaf chameleon, *B. supercil-iaris* (also mentioned earlier) are somewhat more erect and rather gently rounded. This is a large species, attaining an adult size of nearly 4 inches. They have a rather well-defined vertebral ridge and are rather uniformly colored in some shade of brown.

Besides being long, the horned-leaf chameleon is rather deep-bodied and "hefty" for its length.

Both of the above are species of moderate elevations of eastern Madagascar. When cool nighttime (60° to 65°F; 16°–18°C) and day-time (70° to 78°F; 21°–26°C) tempera-tures are provided, these both seem to be hardy chameleon species.

The Pygmy Leaf Chameleon

The tiniest of all chameleons are members of the Malagasy *B. minima* complex. To add to the ongoing con-fusion about changing taxonomy, *B. minima* is now not just a single species but five very similar and very tiny species. At one time, these would have been considered subspecies; now the term "species complex" is preferred. Females (the larger sex) of *B. minima* attain a total length of about 1⅜ inches (3.5 cm). The adult males are typically a quarter of an inch smaller, or about 3 cm. Hatchlings are about five-eighths of an inch (1.5 cm) in total length.

Males typically position themselves on the back of sexually receptive females and are carried about for a day or more. The male of a pair that I kept remained on the back of the female for a full three days.

The minima group seems to be entirely terrestrial in habit. Although they are not difficult to keep, their minuscule size precludes them accept-ing all but the tiniest of food insects,

and obviously their dull coloration takes them out of the category of "flashy" chameleons.

The Armored Leaf Chameleon

Although other leaf chameleons are spiny and "of strange appearance," none equals the amazing *B. perar-mata* in these respects. *Perarmata* imparts none of the feeling of delicacy shown by its congenerics. Instead, it is coarsely scaled, spiny, and tubercu-late, and initially reminds an observer more of Australia's thorny devil or America's horned lizards than a chameleon. In short—it is wonderful!

In color, the armored leaf chameleon is brown of body, limb, and tail with a tan to terra-cotta colored head. The dorsal ridges of the posteriorly directed supraocular crests are serrate. *Perarmata* attains a full 4½ inches (11 cm) in total length.

To date, herpetoculturists have not had much success keeping the armored leaf chameleon in captivity.

Kersten's Leaf Chameleon

The members of the African genus *Rhampholeon* are not often encoun-tered in America's pet trade. Very occasionally a shipment from Tanzania will include a few Kersten's leaf chameleons, *R. kerstenii*.

These are spinose little chameleons that near 3½ inches (9 cm) in length. Like others of the group, they are sub-tly colored in earthen tones, often rus-set or terra-cotta on brown or reddish-brown. Lateral and dorsal striping is often evident (but may be only weakly so). The supraocular crests are anteri-orly directed and a tiny upwardly directed rostral horn is present.

The few of these little chameleons that I have kept have been primarily terrestrial.

They have fed readily on tiny crick-ets and termites and avidly on fruit flies and small houseflies.

Appendix

Photographing Chameleons

Photographing reptiles can be a demanding but fulfilling pursuit. Many hobbyists see photography as the best way to document captive or wild behavior patterns. It is a pursuit that I enjoy immensely. Capturing a chameleon—even a relatively inactive specimen—on film often requires that stealth and field knowledge be combined with the discipline of photography. As you progress, each photo will help you to see how the next could be improved. Getting started is easy.

The equipment required will depend upon a number of variables. Among these are whether you will be taking both long-distance field photos and staged closeups. Of course, since the only chameleon species to become established in the United States, and since none are native here, you will most likely be photographing captive staged specimens. While this is infinitely easier than pursuing and photographing free-ranging specimens, it is not nearly as satisfying.

Some Photographic Hints

For staged photography, create a small natural setting by placing rocks, mosses, leaves, limbs, or bark— whichever is most appropriate for the species you're photographing—on a stage. I use a small lazy Susan as a stage. This enables me to rotate the stage with the animal on it, for different photographic angles. This works well, providing that you move *very slowly*, both in your own actions and in rotating the stage. If you don't have a lazy Susan, just arrange the setting items on a table top or on a tree stump (outdoors or in, depending on where you are at the time), put the lizard in place, focus and shoot. Having a photo assistant to help pose the chameleon will help.

I created a backing for my stage with the top half of a round trash can. I first cut it to size then firmly bolted it in place atop a lazy Susan. Black velvet clipped into place around the inside surface of the background gives a good background for the lizard shots. The result is an easily moved, eminently serviceable stage.

If you are lucky enough to travel to a country in which chameleons are indigenous, I hope you will try your luck at field photography. This can be considerably more trying than staged photography. To accomplish field photography successfully, an assistant is almost a necessity.

When approaching your photographic subject, move very slowly. If you are lucky the creature will remain in place long enough to permit you to get a few shots. You, or your partner, will need to move quickly to capture the specimen if it moves, replace it where you wish to photograph it, then move slowly to refocus and shoot.

Avoid making eye contact with the creature you are hoping to photograph. When the chameleon shows signs of becoming distressed by your approach (as it almost certainly will), freeze for a moment, then begin moving again. Eventually, if you are lucky, you will be close enough to make the field shot for which you were hoping.

Chameleon Imports

In late 1994, Ethan Bright was able to provide summary data regarding the importation of chameleons into the United States. The data was calculated by Bright after being accessed from the importation records of the United States Fish and Wildlife Service by Allen Salzberg of the New York Turtle and Tortoise Society. The figures show why it is so necessary that we learn by our mistakes and strive to make all captive populations of chameleons self-sustaining. Wild populations simply cannot sustain such tremendous numbers being collected without noticeable decline. The figures here, with the exception of those for *Chamaeleo gracilis*, *C. brevicornis*, and the genera *Brookesia* and *Rhampholeon* (estimates of these are by me), are from Ethan Bright (Bright, Ethan. 1994. An analysis of U.S. Fish and Wildlife Service reptile and amphibian numbers in their LEMMIS system. Unpublished.)

The figures reflect numbers imported between January, 1988, and June, 1994. To these conservative figures, I estimate that you may add in the vicinity of 60,000 *C. gracilis*; 300 *C. brevicornis*; 500 *Brookesia* and *Rhampholeon*.

This brings the totals frighteningly near the 200,000 mark, of which but a tiny percentage remain alive. I believe that anyone who truly *likes* animals will agree that changes are in order.

Genus	Species	Quantity	Genus	Species	Quantity
C.	senegalensis	67,457	C.	johnstoni	10,596
C.	dilepis	8,509	C.	lateralis	7,157
C.	pardalis	5,704	C.	jacksonii	4,206
C.	fischeri	4,072	C.	parsonii	4,007
C.	campani	3,303	C.	calyptratus	1,676
C.	oustaleti	1,409	C.	chamaeleon	1,333
C.	montium	1,269	C.	melleri	960
C.	globifer	635	C.	bitaeniatus	551
C.	minor	391	C.	antimena	370
C.	balteatus	367	C.	nasutus	324
C.	willsii	302	C.	verrucosus	300
C.	quadricornis	290	C.	africanus	250
C.	hoehnelii	231	C.	labordi	163
C.	laterispinus	125	C.	fulleborni	100
C.	weidersheimi	100	C.	oshaugnnessyi	81
C.	belalandaensis	80	C.	cristatus	65
C.	marshalli	48	C.	gastrotaenia	36
C.	rudis	35	C.	eisentrauti	33
C.	malthe	27	C.	boettegeri	26
C.	bifidus	25	C.	deremensis	22
C.	rhinoceratus	20	C.	zeylandicus	20
C.	oweni	17	C.	(Bradypodion) thamnobates	12
C.	(Bradypodion) damaranus	7	C.	spinosus	7
C.	pfefferi	6	C.	gallus	5
C.	werneri	4	C.	tenuis	2
C.	namaquensis	1			

Medical Treatments for Parasites

Many chameleons, even those that are captive-bred and hatched, may harbor internal parasites. Because of the complexities of identification of endoparasites and the necessity to accurately weigh specimens to be treated and measure purge dosages, the eradication of internal parasites is best left to a qualified reptile veterinarian. These are a few of the medications and dosages recommended by Richard Funk, D.V.M. Generally, they are based on the weight of the animal.

Amoebas and Trichomonads

Metronidazole, 40–50 mg/kg, orally. The treatment is repeated in 2 weeks.

Dimetridazole can also be used but the dosage is very different. 40–50 mg/kg of Dimetridazole is administered daily for 5 days. The treatment is then repeated in 2 weeks. All treatments with both medications are administered once daily.

Coccidia

Sulfadiazine, sulfamerazine, or sulfamethazine may be administered. The dosages are identical. Give 75 mg/kg the first day, then follow up for the next 5 days with 45 mg/kg. All treatments orally and once daily.

Sulfadimethoxine is also effective. The initial dosage is 90 mg/kg orally to be followed for the next 5 days with 45 mg/kg orally. All dosages are administered once daily.

Trimethoprim-sulfa may also be used. 30 mg/kg should be administered once daily for 7 days.

Cestodes (Tapeworms)

Several effective treatments are available. Bunamidine may be admin-

istered orally at a dosage of 50 mg/kg. A second treatment occurs in 14 days.

Niclosamide, orally, at a dosage of 150 mg/kg, is also effective. A second treatment is given in 2 weeks.

Praziquantel may be administered either orally or intramuscularly. The dosage is 5–8 mg/kg and is to be repeated in 14 days.

Trematodes (Flukes)

Praziquantel at 8 mg/kg may be administered either orally or intramuscularly. The treatment is repeated in 2 weeks.

Nematodes (Roundworms)

Several effective treatments are available.

Levamisole, an injectable intraperitoneal treatment, should be administered at a dosage of 10 mg/kg and the treatment repeated in 2 weeks.

Ivermectin, injected intramuscularly in a dosage of 200 mcg/kg, is effective. The treatment is to be repeated in 2 weeks. Ivermectin can be toxic to certain taxa.

Thiabendazole and Fenbendazole have similar dosages. Both are administered orally at 50–100 mg/kg and repeated in 14 days.

Mebendazole is administered orally at a dosage of 20–25 mg/kg and repeated in 14 days.

Medical Abbreviations Identified

mg	milligram (1 mg = 0.001 gram)
kg	kilogram (1,000 grams; 2.2 pounds)
mcg	microgram (1 mcg = 0.000001 gram)
IM	intramuscularly
IP	intraperitoneally
PO	orally

Useful Literature and Addresses

Addresses

The CHAMELEON Information
  Network
c/o Ken Kalisch
412 West E Street
Encinitas, California 92024
   This is a group of dedicated ama-
teur and professional hobbyists. A
high-quality newsletter is published
sporadically (averages quarterly).

The International Chameleon
  Working Group
c/o Lynn Raw
P.O. Box 200
Merrivale, 3291 South Africa.

   This international group of
chameleon hobbyists publishes
between two and four newsletters
annually.
   There are herpetological clubs
based in many larger cities. Pet
stores, museums, nature centers, and
biology teachers/professors are often
able to advise you of the nearest peer
group.

Books and Articles

Bartlett, Richard. *Properly Caring for
   True Chameleons*. Mission Viejo,
   California; *Reptiles Magazine* 1:1;
   pages 26–33, 1993.

Branch, Bill. *A Field Guide to the
   Snakes and Other Reptiles of
   Southern Africa*. Sanibel, Florida:
   Ralph Curtis Publishing, 1988.

Cowden, Jeanne. *Chameleons, The
   Little Lions of the Reptile World*.
   New York: David McKay, 1977.

Glaw, Frank and Miguel Vences. *A
   Field Guide to the Amphibians and
   Reptiles of Madagascar*. Bonn:
   Privately published, 1994.

LeBerre, Francois. *The New
   Chameleon Handbook*. New York:
   Barron's Educational Series, 1995.

Martin, James. *Masters of Disguise, A
   Natural History of Chameleons*.
   New York: Facts on File, 1992.

McKeown, Sean. *Hawaiian Reptiles
   and Amphibians*. Honolulu: Oriental
   Publishing, 1978.

Preston-Mafham, Ken. *Madagascar, A
   Natural History*. New York: Facts on
   File, 1991.

Schnieper, Claudia. *Chameleons*.
   Minneapolis: Carolrhoda Books,
   1989.

Glossary

aestivation a period of warm-weather inactivity, often triggered by excessive heat or drought

allopatric not occurring together but often adjacent

ambient temperature temperature of the surrounding environment

anterior toward the front

anus external opening of the cloaca; the vent

arboreal tree-dwelling

autotomize the ability to break easily or voluntarily cast off (and usually to regenerate) a part of the body

axillary near the apex (pit) of the arm

bicuspid as used here, pertaining to claws with two points

brumation the reptilian and amphibian equivalent of mammalian hibernation

canthus rostralis (canthal crest) a ridge from beneath the eye to the snout; this may be sharply or gently angled from the plane of the snout

casque the upward projecting cap or helmet at the back of a chameleon's head

caudal pertaining to the tail

chromatophore a pigment-containing skin cell

cloaca the common chamber into which digestive, urinary, and reproductive systems empty and which itself opens exteriorly through the vent or anus

con... as used here, a prefix to several words (generic, specific) indicating "the same" (congeneric refers to species in the same genus, conspecific indicates the same species)

deposition as used here, the laying of the eggs

deposition site the spot chosen by the female to lay her eggs

dermal relating to the skin

diapause a temporary cessation of development, often induced by coolness or dryness

dichromatic two color phases of the same species, often sex-linked

dimorphic a difference in form, build, or coloration involving the same species; often sex-linked

diurnal active in the daytime

dorsal pertaining to the back; upper surface

dorsolateral pertaining to the upper sides

dorsum the upper surface

endemic confined to a specific region

femur the part of the leg between hip and knee

flanks lower side

form an identifiable species or subspecies

fracture planes softer areas in the tail vertebrae which allow the tail to break easily if seized

genus a taxonomic classification of a group of species having similar characteristics (plural: genera)

glossohyal a muscle of the extensible tongue

granular pertaining to small, flat scales

gravid the reptilian equivalent of mammalian pregnancy

gular pertaining to the throat

gular crest a longitudinal ridge of enlarged throat scales

heliothermic pertaining to a species which basks in the sun to thermoregulate

hemipenes the dual copulatory organs of male lizards and snakes

hemipenis the singular form of hemipenes

heterogenous not uniformly sized, colored, or patterned

homogenous uniformly sized, colored, or patterned

horns as used here, referring to the tapered, rigid, often annulated, forward projecting preocular or rostral processes

hybrid offspring resulting from the breeding of two species

hydrate to restore body moisture by drinking or absorption

insular as used here, island-dwelling

intergrade offspring resulting from the breeding of two subspecies

juvenile a young or immature specimen

keel a ridge (along the center of a scale)
keratin the hardened, largely inert, protenaceous outer skin of a reptile

labial pertaining to the lips
lateral pertaining to the side

Malagasy Republic Madagascar
melanism a profusion of black pigment
middorsal pertaining to the middle of the back
midventral pertaining to the center of the belly or abdomen
monotypic containing but one type
montane cool, moist habitat found on the upper slopes of mountain, but terminating below timberline

occipital lobe the flaps or lobes of skin at the rear of some chameleons heads
ocelli light, centered rings
ontogenetic changes changes occurring during growth
ontogeny the course of development
oviparous reproducing by means of eggs that hatch after laying
ovoviviparous reproducing by means of shelled or membrane-contained eggs that hatch prior to, or at deposition

parietal eye a sensory organ present in certain reptiles which is positioned midcranially
phalanges the bones of the toes
poikilothermic a species with no internal body temperature regulation (the old term was "cold-blooded")
posterior toward the rear
prehensile grasping
preocular anterior to the eye

race a subspecies
rostral pertaining to the nose area
rugose not smooth; wrinkled or tuberculate

saxicolous rock-dwelling
scansorial capable of, or adapted for climbing
serrate saw-like
species a group of similar creatures that produce viable young when breeding
subcaudal beneath the tail
subdigital beneath the toes
subspecies the subdivision of a species. A race that may differ slightly in color, size, scalation, or other criteria
sympatric occurring together

tarsal spur an outgrowth on the heel
taxonomy the science of classification of plants and animals
terrestrial land-dwelling
thermoregulate to regulate (body) temperature by

choosing a warmer or cooler environment
thigmothermic pertaining to a species (often nocturnal) which thermoregulates by being in contact with a preheated surface such as a boulder or tarred road surface
tubercles warty protuberances
tuberculate pertaining to tubercles
tympanum the external eardrum

vent the external opening of the cloaca; the anus
venter the underside of a creature; the belly
ventral pertaining to the undersurface or belly
ventrolateral pertaining to the sides of the venter (belly)
vertebral pertaining to the middorsal area
vertebral crest a ridge of scales or an actual longitudinal middorsal crest

Note: Other scientific definitions are contained in the following two volumes:

Peters, James A. *Dictionary of Herpetology*. New York: Hafner Publishing, 1964.

Wareham, David C. *The Reptile and Amphibian Keeper's Dictionary*. London: Blandford, 1993.

Index

Numbers in **boldface** type indicate color photos.